U.S. Lifestyles and Mainline Churches

U.S. Lifestyles and Mainline Churches

A Key to Reaching People in the 90's

Tex Sample

WESTMINSTER/JOHN KNOX PRESS
Louisville, Kentucky

© 1990 Tex Sample

Scripture quotations are from the Revised Standard Version of the Bible, copyrighted 1946, 1952, © 1971, 1973 by the Division of Christian Education of the National Council of the Churches of Christ in the U.S.A., and are used by permission.

Book design by Polebridge Press, Inc.

First edition

Published by Westminster/John Knox Press
Louisville, Kentucky

PRINTED IN THE UNITED STATES OF AMERICA

9   8   7   6   5   4   3

Library of Congress Cataloging-in-Publication Data

Sample, Tex.
  U.S. lifestyles and mainline churches : a key to reaching people
in the 90's / Tex Sample. — 1st ed.
      p.   cm.
  Includes bibliographical references.
  ISBN 0-664-25099-8

  1. United States—Church history—20th century.   2. United States—
Civilization—20th century.   3. Religion and sociology—United
States—History—20th century.   I. Title.
BR526.S25   1990
270'.0973'09049—dc20   89-48300
                                                                  CIP

Dedicated to
Shawn Sanford Sample
Jennifer Jo Sample Butler

And in memory of
Steven Barry Sample

Contents

Acknowledgments

I am deeply indebted to a great many people who made this book possible. Here I need to express appreciation to some of them by name.

I want to thank the trustees, administration, and faculty of Saint Paul School of Theology for a sabbatical leave in the fall and winter of the 1988–89 academic year, when most of the writing of the book was done. Special thanks are due to President Lovett H. Weems, Jr., and Academic Dean Eleanor Scott Meyers for their sustained encouragement and hearty support.

My faculty colleague Eugene L. Lowry did a careful reading of the first draft of this manuscript, and Susan Ruach did as well, especially the chapters dealing with the cultural left. They saved me from not a few serious errors and misstatements.

Kathleen Campbell, as my student assistant, chased down hundreds of references, prepared bibliographies, and worked through several libraries in town. She also did a meticulous proofreading of the final draft. Her extraordinarily high-quality work is deeply appreciated.

Betty Barton transcribed a number of my lectures and typed several first-draft chapters. I thank her for both her assistance and her friendship for the past twenty-two years.

Lydia Cantrill typed and retyped several drafts of the manuscript with her usual good spirit. She also contributed a steady commentary on lifestyle issues out of her own experience, from which I learned continually. I thank her for her hard work and good-hearted support.

Harold Twiss served as editor of the manuscript, the second time it has been my good fortune to work with him. His motivating support, his careful eye for clarity, and his wise suggestions have made this a better book than I can write.

My spouse, Peggy, is the dearest friend in my life. I thank her for an ecology of love and care. The book is dedicated to our children, Shawn and Jennifer, and to the memory of Steven. Baby boomers, they instructed me as much as anyone.

With help as generous and capable as I have received, I have no one to blame for the problems that remain except myself.

U.S. Lifestyles
and Mainline
Churches

Introduction

Mary is from Kansas City, where her parents live, and now works and makes her home in St. Louis. She and Mike live together there without benefit of clergy. This arrangement is a matter of no little consternation on the part of her mother and father. In fact, her lifestyle has been a problem for them since she reached her teens. Now thirty years old and not married, Mary has no plans for the immediate future much different from the present pattern of her life. She has not settled on a career, and neither has Mike. She sees herself as living out her own agenda and refuses to settle into some "rut" because of the expectations of others. While she is not affluent, Mary did graduate from college, but she and Mike so far have turned away from pursuing careers in the way their fathers had done. Mary's failure to make career plans and her unwillingness to commit herself to marriage simply baffle her parents. This, plus the fact that she does not go to church, leaves them wondering how they failed her. While they often argue with her and beg her to be sensible, down deep they believe that the fault is finally theirs. While they are a very successful family, they feel that somehow they have been failures as parents.

Last fall Mary called home from St. Louis.

"Mom, Mike and I want to come home for a visit."

"Oh, you are going to—ah—bring . . . Mike. Well, that's fine. He can sleep in the guest room."

"Mother, Mike and I sleep together all the time. We can just stay in my old room."

"Not in this house, you won't!"

"Mother, don't be antediluvian."

"My dear, in this house there has never been a flood!"

"All right, all right, have it your way, but we really do need to have time to talk. You see, Mom, I'm pregnant."

Silence, then: "Oh, my, then you and Mike want to talk about getting married?"

"Well, no, Mom, we don't intend to get married at this point."

"Then you want to talk about getting an abortion?"

"No, Mother, we want to talk about keeping the baby."

"Oh, my, my, my."

3

When Mary's mother hung up the phone, her first thought was how to tell her husband, but then she worried about how she would tell Mary's grandparents. Her parents and her husband's parents still live in a small town in rural Missouri. Hardworking, wage-earning people, they made great sacrifices to get their children through college and now draw enormous pride from their success. They are the backbone of their local church and are deeply committed to traditional values and morality.

"It will just kill them when they find out," Mary's mother said to herself, "and there is no way to keep it from them."

This true story is a glimpse at what this book is about: three broad but sharply different lifestyles that presently characterize the population of the United States. I call them the cultural left, the cultural middle, and the cultural right. The cultural left is made up largely of inner-directed, self-fulfillment baby boomers, who are now in their twenties, thirties, and early forties. Their lifestyle is a radical departure from that of all previous generations in the United States. Mary and Mike are representative of this group in the story above, and this lifestyle is discussed in Part Two.

The cultural middle is constituted of those successful business and professional people who are career-oriented and seek to make it to the top. They are fulfillers of the American dream and live out—or strive to—the established values of the dominant culture. Mary's parents reflect this lifestyle, which is the subject of Part Four.

The grandparents come from the cultural right, the largest lifestyle group of the three. They are self-denying local people who hold tenaciously to traditional values and conventional morality. Their lifestyle is even more distant from the cultural left, which most do not understand and which many vigorously oppose. These folk are the concern of Part Three. In Part Five I shall address the question of how a local church can work with such diverse lifestyles in the same congregation, and I shall suggest a theological stance appropriate to indigenous lifestyle ministry.

It is important to understand that in using a left, middle, and right spectrum, I am not talking about political positions but about lifestyles. While the cultural left is politically the most liberal of the group, the parallel ends there, as we shall see. Moreover, one can be culturally left and politically right, or vice versa. Each cultural group is politically diverse, so that one cannot simply infer a political point of view from a particular lifestyle. Tendencies, however, do exist. As the cultural left tends to be more liberal, the cultural middle is the most politically conservative, with the cultural right more moderate, although here too sizable minorities will vary from the general political tendencies each lifestyle possesses.

A further word of clarification. The story about Mary and Mike may seem to suggest that these lifestyles are strictly generational. While it is true that a large number of baby boomers are in the cultural left, many baby boomers are also in the cultural middle or right. Moreover, older U.S. citizens are by no means all culturally right. In fact, some are no doubt on the cultural left. The point is that these lifestyles can be quite complex generationally.

Furthermore, lifestyle issues are desperately important for mainline churches, whose memberships come almost exclusively from the cultural middle and the cultural right. These churches have shown a serious inability to reach those on the cultural left and a large group in the cultural middle and right. If mainline churches are to reverse the precipitous membership decline of the past two decades, this problem must be addressed.

Another issue concerns the church's capacity to deal sensitively and respectfully with the different lifestyles in the United States. Mainline churches with an educated clergy are becoming increasingly middle class in worship, preaching, program, and outreach. Such an approach is not adequate to meet the diversity of people in U.S. culture and leaves mainline churches to focus on a minority—albeit a sizable one—of the U.S. population. To turn toward other lifestyles will require something more than merely tinkering with program. An appreciation for and a decided interest in these people will be necessary. Without such focus and concern, mainline churches will continue to shrink in membership.

The problem, however, is deeper than this. What is at stake here is the direction of U.S. culture and the question of whether mainline churches will influence the shape of the future. In spite of all the publicity given to conservative and fundamentalist churches in recent years, they are not drawing any greater proportion of the population and are not reversing the trends in the United States.[1] In fact, it is extraordinarily unlikely that they can reach the people at the front edge of cultural change. Mainline churches have a better chance to do so. The questions are: *Can* mainline churches find vision and identity in their present muddle of confusion and low morale, and *will* mainline churches commit themselves to learning and responding to the diverse groups that make up this society?

Finally, it is not enough to reach people. Hitler reached people. Life-and-death issues confront this society and this planet. The way theology and ethics are done in mainline churches is too greatly conditioned by the styles of university and seminary discourse. I realize that some pastors drop their training and their study habits soon after seminary, but I am not focusing on the indolent, at least not here. I am concerned about those who *are* informed and highly motivated to do

theology and ethics and who are committed to critical reflection on the
mission of the church in the world. Their approach to theology and to
issues is vastly different from that of a large number of Americans. To be
able to do the critical and constructive task of theology and social ethics
in an approach indigenous to lifestyles in the United States is a major
challenge for those committed to a gospel of grace for the liberation and
transformation of life on this planet. This concern is paramount in what
follows.

► Part One ◄

*Diversity and
Change in
U.S. Lifestyles*

▶1◀

Shifting Values: Self–Fulfillment vs. Self–Denial

I can remember a time when I did not know what a baby boomer was. I was born at the very end of 1934, so I was eleven years old in 1946 when the first baby boomers came along. Life was different then. I loved baseball, but we had no Little League and had to "prepare" our own ball diamonds. We took lawn mowers to cut base paths in a pasture and used cow chips for first, second, third, and home plate.

John Smiley was an older guy, but he was small and preferred to play ball with us younger kids. Being older, he was also smarter, so he would organize a team with all the good players and challenge the rest of us to a game. I remember once that they beat us 69 to 11, and I pitched two innings of shutout ball in that game!

When I turned twenty, twenty-one, twenty-two years of age, suddenly there were Little Leagues everywhere, and later there would be Babe Ruth leagues, American Legion, and other youth programs. Then, as the baby boomers grew older, there were softball leagues for adults. The baby boomers had come of baseball age. In 1950, for example, there were 776 organizations of Little League baseball. In 1960 there were 5,700.[1]

Suddenly, schools that used to house us were overwhelmed, and the country turned to raising this mammoth generation. I then began to understand what it was like to live a decade in front of a tidal wave of human flesh that would affect every aspect of my life from that time on.

In the 60's many boomers let their hair grow long and wore bib overalls, an apparel spurned by my generation, a good number of whom swore that if they ever got out of those insufferable things they would never wear them again. But for boomers they sometimes appeared to be formal attire.

In the mid-60's I turned thirty, and I heard something I had never heard before in my whole life: "Don't trust anybody over thirty." Guess who was under thirty?

A few years back I spent the night in the bedroom of a college sophomore. She was away at school, and her parents, my friends, let me stay there one night. With my sociological interests I did archival research; I read her walls. On one corkboard was a postcard that read, DON'T TRUST ANYBODY UNDER SIXTEEN. The card had a 1980 date on it. This was the year the last of the boomers turned sixteen.

For at least ten years I suffered through the middle-age crazies, and most of the women my age that I knew were struggling with or had struggled with menopause, but the boomers are just now coming into these marvelous mid-life maladies. If you think you have heard about middle-age crazies and menopause before, just wait. As the boomers, who at 76.4 million represent nearly one person in three in our society, begin to experience these mid-life assaults, you will think they are the first ever to endure such derangement.

I will turn sixty-five just three days before the year 2000. The baby boomers begin to retire about a decade later, and they will reach sixty-five from 2011 until 2029. They will challenge the retirement systems, pensions, and Social Security as these have never been challenged before. Yet as a block of some 70 million voters, they will have an electoral power unprecedented by the aged in the history of the nation.[2]

Baby boomers have affected us in so many ways. Because they are such a large generation, everyone wants to sell them something. In the aftermath of this marketing project are strewn mountainous trash heaps of hula hoops, coonskin caps à la Davy Crockett, Barbie dolls, Beatles records, drug paraphernalia, beads, and jeans, jeans, jeans. A few years back, country singer and writer Tom T. Hall said he was no longer going to write and record music for his generation—that's *my* generation—but would turn his attention to the younger people (the baby boomers). When asked why, he observed that they are the ones who buy the records and the tapes.

This comes from the man who wrote "Old Dogs, Little Children, and Watermelon Wine." This is serious!

The politicians continue to seek a way to gel and to win the baby boomer vote. In the election year of 1988, however, the boomer vote showed no sign of being corralled, and the political and electoral quest for their support goes on.

The point of all this is that the baby boomers have had a massive impact on U.S. society and will continue to do so as the nation's largest generation well into the twenty-first century. They will influence your life and mine—whether you are a boomer or not—as long as we live.

Moreover, there is perhaps no point at which their weight has been felt more than in the operative values and norms of the society. The new ethic of the baby boomers represents a fundamental alteration of the values and norms that informed most of the American people during the first two hundred years of U.S. history. It is this shift toward a new ethic that is, perhaps, the most powerful change the boomers have brought to our national life. It is important to realize that most baby boomers have not espoused this new ethic, at least not in its strongest expressions, but some 30 million have. In order to see the impact of this lifestyle change, we need to look first at the ethic in place when the boomers came on the scene.

Self-Denial

Before the baby boomers the ethic that informed most people in the United States throughout their nearly two-hundred-year history was what Daniel Yankelovich has termed "the self-denial ethic." In a 1981 study he found that most Americans continue to hold to this ethic, although it has been challenged by the new ethic of cultural-left baby boomers. The sharp contradiction between this traditional set of values and those of the baby boomers can be seen by a close look at Yankelovich's findings.[3]

The ethic of self-denial has three basic parts. The first of these is the understanding that one denies self for the sake of the security and well-being of the family. Whatever it takes to provide for the family and its needs and to keep it together, one does.

I was raised in a self-denial family. My mother and father, quite simply, were prepared to do virtually anything that was good for my sister, Pat, and me. In the eighth grade I had the world by the tail. I was on the fourth string of the high school football team. (We were basically cannon fodder for the third team.) I was the sports editor and columnist for the two-page eighth-grade newspaper known as *Behind the Eight Ball*, and I was, most of all, madly in love with the girl who would in a brief two years be the drum majorette of the Brookhaven High School Panther Band. All this, mind you, in a football and majorette culture.

Then it began to happen. My feet went flat, and I had to get arch supports. My eyes went bad, and I had to get glasses. About the same time I noticed that when I ran into—notice I did *not* say tackled—one of those third-team running backs, I had these terrible spasms in my lower back, called slipped discs. When my folks took me to the "bone doctor," he told me I had spondylolisthesis, basically a condition in which the top of your spine does not sit straight on the vertebrae down at your hips. Putting me in an armchair back brace that went from my hips to just under my arms, he told me to come back next summer for a fusion (which I never did). The brace made me feel like a freak, and, of course, I had to quit football. In the doctor's gentle words, "If you don't, you'll probably paralyze yourself for life" (which I never did).

Then it got worse: I got acne! I don't mean a few pimples here and there. I had the number-one case of acne in all of Mississippi. I could walk down the street and people would say, "He's Number One!"

Finally, I lost my girl to a football player. Well, my life had just come to an end, or so it seemed.

My father and mother were the owners of the 13 Taxi Company (called "13" because that was the phone number). In 1949 they were $4,000 in debt to the bank, which was about all the business was worth, but the bank would always lend them money because they knew my folks would pay it back. My parents borrowed another $500 and bought for me a 1940 Ford coupe, which they gave me as I turned fifteen. What a car! Streamlined with those swept-back fenders and a hood that looked like the bow of a ship, it still had both running boards, and I put a fifteen-foot aerial on it with the American flag flying at the top. Even though it was a coupe, it had two flop-down seats just behind the front one. My buddy, Bobby Gaskill, liked to sit on the one on the right side because he chewed Beech-Nut chewing tobacco. There was a tear in the upholstery over there, and he could spit down the hole. You could turn a corner in that car and it would go *gurgle-gurgle*.

Knowing that my parents were in a business debt of crisis proportions, I simply could not understand why they had borrowed more money to buy the car. I used to ask my mother why.

"Mama, you and Dad are in debt, and yet you borrowed money to buy that car. Why?"

She never would tell me the whole truth. Rather, she simply said the same thing over and over: "Well, son, you need something to go see the dermatologist in."

Much later, after I was thirty-five years old, I cornered her in the kitchen and finally got the truth.

"Mama, I want to know, really—why did you go into debt to buy me that car?"

"Son, so much was going bad with you that we were afraid you would run from life, and we wanted to give you something that would keep you in the middle of the street."

This is self-denial. In this ethic is an abiding commitment to sacrifice and a conviction that immediate gratification is to be postponed for the sake of long-term gain, especially when that gain serves the family, one's child, one's spouse. Such self-denial was understood as the way the world was. In the same way that it was required for what Yankelovich calls familial success, it was also necessary for one's job or career. Reality simply had to be negotiated by means of self-denial. To do otherwise was to build a house on the highly granulated, moving ground of immediate gratification, a dwelling unstable in the hardships and storms of life as most Americans had known it.

Deeply related to this self-denial for the sake of the family was the understanding, says Yankelovich, that one worked hard—and had to—to provide for the necessities of life. Making a living, making ends meet, trying to get ahead but not making much progress—these were the experiences of the overwhelming majority of the American people. Luxuries, if there were any at all, came after the necessities. My mother-in-law captures it in a phrase I've heard, symbolically, a thousand times: "Well, you work hard to pay for the necessities and hope you have enough left over for a few luxuries."

The third ingredient in this ethic of self-denial was respectability. To have a good home, to have children who were well-behaved, who did not bring discredit or scandal to the family, to be able to "hold one's head up in the community"—all of these were badges of family success.

I can remember as an adolescent that we would be home, my mother and I, and the windows would be down, the doors closed, and the neighbors' houses would be 75 feet away on either side, but my mother would *still* be whispering. "Son, whatever you do, please don't get some little girl pregnant. Why, it would ruin your life; it would ruin your sister's life. We couldn't stay in this town." (Mama was worried about my getting somebody pregnant, when I was doing all I could just to kiss somebody!)

Closely related was her attitude toward the school. "Son, when I go up to the school I don't want to hear that you've been misbehaving. When I go up to the school, I don't want this family embarrassed." To my mother and my father the school was always "up." It did not matter that the route to the school was virtually downhill all the way—to Mom and Dad it was *up*. The school, along with the church, was the institutional setting where the proof of one's respectability was gained.

Please do not misunderstand. Neither my mother nor my father was uptight or highly repressed, although a good deal of that went on in the culture of self-denial. For them, as for the overwhelming majority of Americans, success was denied them in terms of the culture's expectations of getting to the top and, more recently, of being Number One. Very few people, if any, could win in the Horatio Alger sense, especially nonwhites and women.

The point is that in a success-oriented culture, where the ideal is denied virtually to all, compensative values will be necessary, and in the self-denial ethic of the United States respectability was the dominant value for offsetting the sense of self-loss and failure one experienced when caught between achievement myths and social realities.[4]

My concern here is that we deal tenderly with these kinds of issues. Those who hold the self-denial ethic are as courageous, as complex, as interested in living deeply and well as perhaps any other generation, but the social context of U.S. society was different for those born in the first half of this century than for those born in the last half. The self-denial people of today have two major events that permanently shaped their consciousness: the Great Depression and World War II. When the stock market crashed in 1929, the ethic of self-denial faced a bitter test, and in terms of the sheer capacity to hunker down and survive, it served well those generations who knew the Depression's deprivation and emptying.

Before the Depression had ended, the United States engaged in world war for the second time in a quarter century. The country went through nearly four years of the separation, terror, and death of "the good war."

No one over fifty years of age in this society has escaped the impact of these two events. One's memory and the way one anticipates the future, the hard lessons learned in confronting seemingly intractable events with their tragedy and pathos, and finally, at least as perceived, the coming of victory over them—these have stained the participants forever. The cognitive, emotional, and valuing frameworks by which "reality" is appropriated have been stamped indelibly by these two encompassing, historical episodes in the national life. The self-denial called out and given in response has proved itself, beyond doubt, as the ethic that, at the minimum, must undergird lifestyles less tested and tempered in the duress and struggle of a world that, finally, is not one's oyster, rose garden, or playground.

Self-Fulfillment

When the war ended, the people of the United States had known either depression or war for sixteen years. Those returning from the war and those who had remained home seemed determined to put life together again. Women were encouraged to leave or were pushed out of the nontraditional jobs they had held during the war effort, and the growing movement for racial justice had not yet broken loose. The emphasis was clearly on making up for lost time: having a family and getting on with life. Veterans' benefits and F.H.A. loans provided for the construction of homes in unprecedented numbers. The suburbanization of the country began. While poverty continued to stalk a large number of Americans, crescendoing up to 22 percent of the American people in 1960, the United States entered into a period of affluence unknown in the past. The average family income more than doubled in constant dollars in the years between 1950 and 1973.[5] In this postwar fervor, most

American parents committed themselves to providing for their children all the things that they never had.

On January 1, 1946, at one second after midnight in Philadelphia, Pennsylvania, Kathleen Casey was born. The first baby boomer had arrived. For the next eighteen years the baby boomers not only brought the nation its largest generation in history but also a radically different ethic from that of self-denial. Out of 76.4 million baby boomers, some 30 million of them would be deeply committed to this new ethic.

Yankelovich has named it an ethic of self-fulfillment. A number of ingredients give some sense of its mood and makeup. In the first place this ethic maintains that life is intrinsically valuable, which means that it is not to be denied for the sake of something else, and self-denial is one instance of such. Life is not to be denied for the sake of family, career, country, or anything else; rather, these are to fit, if they can, into a self-fulfilling lifestyle.[6]

One baby boomer told this story: "When I was growing up, my father used to tell me what a great pension he had. He said, 'We may not have everything we want now and may not be able to do all the things we'd like, but when I retire, we are going to be able to have and do all we've waited for.' Well, he worked for that corporation for forty years, and when he retired he got the gold watch and, sure enough, a nice pension, but he died after the first six months. Now, there were medical reasons for why my father died, but those weren't the real reasons. My father died because he could not live without putting off life. . . . That's just not going to happen to me. I intend to live."

Yankelovich calls this yearning for the intrinsic value of life the "sacred/expressive" aspect of the self-fulfillment ethic. He means "sacred" not so much in the religious sense or in contrast to the secular but in opposition to an instrumental orientation. For baby boomers with a self-fulfillment ethic, it is not enough for something to be a means to something else; it needs to be worthwhile in and of itself.[7]

Second, in the self-fulfillment ethic, life is to be creatively and emotionally expressive. Growing up in affluence and in the expanding economy of the 50's, 60's, and early 70's, children saw how their parents had made a life for themselves through hard work and self-denial, but they also saw the constricted choices and the life-blunting effects of these choices. To these baby boomers, an ethic braced by the hardships of depression and war was not adequate for the range of options opening before them in their own experience. Yankelovich reports how impressed he was in his studies of the student revolt of the 60's with "how extensively students identified with the suppressed elements in their parents' lives."[8] From the beginning most baby boomers were troubled by the split in U.S. life between a public and a private self, the first operating according to utilitarian individualism in the workaday world and the second seeking in individual expression a haven in private life where the self's own claims could be met.[9]

For those who sought self-fulfillment most, expressive individualism took precedence over the more traditional utilitarian form.

This development brought with it a wide range of instructions, mottoes, and counterculture wisdom heard over the past twenty-five years: "Let it all hang out"; "You only go round once in life, so live it with all the gusto you can"; "You have to do what's right for you"; "The individual has to make up his or her own mind"; "Do it now"; "Enjoy"; "I'm not in this world to live up to your expectations and you're not in this world to live up to mine; but if we find each other, it's beautiful"; and so on. These are the comments of a generation profoundly committed to individual creativity and emotional openness, honesty, and self-revelation.

A third set of characteristics of the baby boomers Yankelovich captured with what he termed the psychology of affluence. Formed in the expanding economy of postwar America, this pattern has at least four aspects. The first is the notion that an individual is entitled to affluence; it is a basic right that society owes to everyone. Second, the economy can and will continue to provide the cornucopia of goods and services necessary to guarantee that right; the economy works automatically. Third, when asked what they want, Yankelovich found that baby boomers most deeply committed to the self-fulfillment ethic answered "More." Finally, the psychology of affluence maintains that fulfillment of the self is a basic lifelong project. Indeed, one has a moral obligation to fulfill the self. It is the basic calling of one's life.[10]

An acquaintance of mine who is a lay person in a local church where I occasionally speak heard me summarize Yankelovich's description of the psychology of affluence and headed toward me at the end of the session. An ex-minor league baseball player who wears a bejeweled American flag in his lapel and has a middle-aged bulge of a stomach that obviously cost him a lot of money, he began half shouting his thoughts from across the room.

"Hey, Tex, boy, I know what you're talking about. I really do. I got me one of those baby boomers. I mean he's just like that psychology of affluence.

"You know what he's doin'?" He didn't wait for an answer. "He's going to veterinary school. Yeah, it costs me twelve thousand bucks a year to send that boy to school.

"You know what he did the other day? He called me on the phone and told me he was tired of living in a slum. I said to him, 'Well, son, it may be a slum to you, but I call it a college dormitory.' He said, 'Aw,

Dad, it's a slum; it's awful. I want to get an apartment.' 'Not on my twelve thou,' I said. [By now my friend was shouting.] He said, 'Now, wait a minute, Dad, I've got an idea that won't cost any more money. You see, this other student wants to go in with me and rent a place together.' 'Not on my twelve thousand,' I insisted, figuring he didn't need all that. And do you know what he said? 'Aw, Dad, come on. I want to do it, and *she* wants to do it.' That did it. I exploded. *'Not on my twelve thousand!'"*

It is important to realize that not all baby boomers hold to the self-fulfillment ethic in its strongest expression. For one sizable group self-fulfillment is a way of life, one they are deeply committed to, hence the strong form. Other boomers, who are influenced by it but not so devoted to it, represent the "weak" form, as Yankelovich labels it. He reports that 17 percent of the U.S. people have the "strong form of self-fulfillment."[11] About 63 percent of the population have the ethic in the weaker form. Other concerns such as family, work, or the social norms governing sexuality, marriage, women, heterosexual and homosexual issues, and the rest may be questioned, and self-fulfillment functions as part of this matrix of concerns, but the ethic of self-fulfillment is not the major factor. Yankelovich also reports on a group of about "20 percent or so of adult Americans" who remain "unaffected in their philosophy of life" by this new ethic. Conservative in cultural outlook, these are old people, often rural; they include some of those who are poor, both black and white Americans.[12]

Yet the baby boomers have been the generation most characterized by the ethic of self-fulfillment, and they, more than any other group, can be identified as its primary carriers. Whether in the strong form, which I will characterize later as the core of the cultural left, or those baby boomers more in Yankelovich's mainstream, the cultural middle, they have been profoundly affected by the self-fulfillment ethic.

Now consider this: The generation missing from the mainline denominations is this group of young adults in their twenties, thirties, and early forties, and the basic reason for the decline of the mainline denominations is that this generation, alienated from major institutions in the society, simply dropped out of the church. The fact is that the more strongly one holds to an ethic of self-fulfillment, the less likely one is to belong to the church. The result is that churches are filled primarily with people committed to a self-denial ethic, which poses the direct challenge of how a church of self-denial people can attract self-fulfillment baby boomers. Aggravating this problem further is the fact that people in these two lifestyles see things so differently, approach life so disparately, and evaluate matters so oppositely that it can be extraordinarily difficult to get them together.[13]

I was speaking in a local church and describing these two lifestyles. As I indicated how important it was for the church to reach out to this generation, I was interrupted by one person who said, "Well, we will be glad to have these people in our church when they become Christian. It says in scripture that if one is to do that one must deny himself, take up the cross, and follow Christ." Miraculously, *one* baby boomer was present, and she jumped in immediately. "It also says that Christ came that we might have life and have it more abundantly." I have never seen the issue more sharply put than that in a local church.

Pose the question this way: What will happen to mainline churches, given the average age of most congregations, if there is not some significant infusion of the baby boom generation? Literally thousands of local churches have memberships with an average age above fifty. Where will they be in twenty years?

Yet another concern has to do with American culture itself. If the church cannot draw to itself a large number of baby boomers, especially those who represent the secularizing edge of our culture and where it is going, how will the church influence and help to shape the society of the twenty-first century?

And, finally—for now—if the church sees itself as committed to a transformative role in the world, how can it affect a generation—and, perhaps soon, a society—with which it has little relationship, except to those who hold traditional values?

In the midst of this kind of discussion, of course, the question arises as to why mainline churches are declining while conservative churches are growing. People observe that these conservative churches certainly have baby boomers; and they *do*, but there is a very important difference. Until the coming of the baby boomers, mainline churches were able to draw the young college-educated people of the nation. For previous generations mainline churches, as Hoge and Roozen have demonstrated, provided a bridge between traditional Christianity rooted institutionally in the churches and secular humanistic culture based in the scientific and intellectual establishment, especially higher education. This bridge, however, has now collapsed. College-educated, cosmopolitan, affluent, middle-class young people—the baby boomers—who prized individual expression, freedom, autonomy, and relativism simply left the churches. In their religious journeys their religious expression was noninstitutional, mystical-therapeutic, and experimental.[14] The loss of these young adults cut off mainline churches from a major source of members and future leaders.

Conservative churches, however, have drawn their memberships dominantly from the traditional wing of our society, which I shall later describe as the cultural right. While mainline churches have also drawn from this end of the continuum and still do, it was only one source. They drew also from the great middle and cultural left. As the baby boomers of both the left and the middle dropped out of the churches in large numbers, those on the cultural right stayed for the most part and continued traditional patterns of church membership and attendance. This meant that conservative churches have benefited from the numerical impact of the baby boomers on the cultural right and right of middle. Many of those Americans on the right side of the culture have reacted against the self-fulfillment ethic: the autonomy, the relativism, and the excessive—in their view—personal freedom, not to mention the new morality, the feminist movement, gay/lesbian rights, the attacks on Americanism, abortion, the banning of prayer in public schools, and so on. Many conservative churches—not all—have been fueled by this reaction, producing a highly committed membership, strengthened and reinforced by tradition-oriented baby boomers.

To put it crisply, mainline churches lost the baby boomers of the cultural left and middle in massive numbers. The cultural shift in values cut them off from what had been major sources of new members. Meanwhile, the conservative churches saw no interruption of the flow of members because their cultural-right baby boomers continued their patterns of church attendance and support for cultural-right values and lifestyle.

The 80's: A Time of Economic Reversal

Yankelovich's study captured the baby boomers at the end of the 70's, but even then he saw basic shifts occurring among them. For one thing, economic reversals that had begun in the mid-70's were having their effect, making it very difficult to follow a psychology of affluence when the economy was turning sour. Inflation, the increasing cost of oil and gas, the growing imbalance of payments, defense expenditures, the decline of U.S. productivity and competitiveness, the aging of tools and industrial capacity, and so on have brought financial duress to many baby boomers and a growing sense that they will be the first generation of Americans to have less than their parents had.[15]

Economic hardship for baby boomers continued throughout the 80's no matter what changes the Reagan administration brought by reducing inflation and enhancing the economic benefits of the affluent and wealthy. For example, in 1987 the national United Way study on the future reported that 72 percent of the baby boomers average $10,000 per year in income.[16]

It is understandable why so many baby boomers believe that it takes two incomes to make it in our society. However, these hard times are not likely to end soon. Before 1980 every American owed about $3,000 on the national debt. By 1988 every child born in the United States owed $63,000 on the national debt when she or he drew first breath.[17] Economic problems of this magnitude are likely to be with us for some time. It is little wonder that Yankelovich found that many baby boomers were unable to afford a psychology of affluence.

Another of Yankelovich's findings was that baby boomers were realizing that nothing so destroyed self-fulfillment as self-indulgence. The latter had not served baby boomers well and, in fact, had proved nearly fatal in the quest for a meaningful and viable lifestyle.[18]

In 1981 Yankelovich reported that he saw in the data what he thought were the beginnings of a new trend. New changes were on the way. He projected the emergence of "a new ethic of commitment." In this ethic he saw baby boomers continuing to hold to the outlook that life is intrinsically valuable and is meant to be creatively and emotionally expressive. Indeed, these have continued to be an important part of the boomer lifestyle. The other major aspect of the self-fulfillment ethic, that of the psychology of affluence, was slipping away.

In place of the psychology of affluence were two important new directions, which, as we shall see, do characterize baby boomers now and are supported by other research. The first of these was the search by baby boomers for deeper and more lasting relationships. The stress on self-fulfillment with its "do your own thing" character in the 60's became "I have a duty to myself" in the 70's, but both had the same stultifying and truncating effect. Both lead inevitably to loneliness and to the shrinkage of the self. One baby boomer said it well. "I have just spent too much of my life enjoying all the sights and sounds I could, but I'm thirty-eight years old and I've never found the person I want to spend my life with. I doubt that I've got the kind of deep friendships I can count on. I've just decided I don't want to grow old and be lonely." This is increasingly the testimony of the generation. But let it be clear: They want life to be valuable and worthwhile, and they want it to be emotionally rich and expressive. Moreover, the more education they have, the more individualistic they will tend to be. In the midst of this, however, they know vividly now that the intrinsic value of life and its emotionally expressive possibilities will not happen apart from deep and lasting relationships.

The second trend Yankelovich saw emerging was that baby boomers increasingly wanted to give themselves to something important, something that counted. They wanted to advance society as well as the self. Baby boomers realized that self-fulfillment required commitments, and baby boomers, less self-absorbed, were more prepared to commit themselves to realistic, necessary tasks amid the toughening economic realities of the 80's. This commitment, moreover, extended to the wider society itself. Yankelovich did not see this trend in place but rather saw what he thought was the beginning of a new direction.[19]

We can turn now to more recent studies as we look at changes among baby boomers. Specifically we will look at the baby boomers most committed to self-fulfillment and inner direction, the large lifestyle group I call the cultural left.

►Part Two◄

The
Cultural
Left

▶2◀

Who Are the Cultural Left?

Most baby boomers are not on the cultural left, and this lifestyle includes some who are not baby boomers. Yet some 33 million people in the United States are cultural left, and the overwhelming majority of these are baby boomers. As we have seen, this cultural left represents a substantial break with the self-denial lifestyles of the past in the United States. Their self-fulfillment ethic views life as intrinsically valuable and as emotionally expressive. Furthermore, over the last decade cultural-left baby boomers sought deeper and more lasting relationships and committed themselves to issues that count toward a more just, sustainable, and peaceable society.

With this introduction in place we can turn to a more explicit characterization of the cultural left. The first is their strong inner direction, in contrast to the outer direction typical of U.S. Americans of previous generations. These baby boomers reacted sharply to the conformism they witnessed in their parents as they grew up. Often they saw parents working at jobs they did not really like, staying in marriages with spouses they did not love for the sake of the children, living in accord with community standards they did not actually agree with, and committing themselves to churches that were not finally compelling in belief and action. Rejecting these outer-directed allegiances of their parents, they determined that they would address the world from an inner direction, turning to a kind of internal gyroscope for a more subjective and autonomous guide for personal life. With this came a refusal to abide by traditional "oughts" and "shoulds." The obligations of community, business, family, country, and faith failed to capture the commitment of most baby boomers, especially the cultural left.

A second characteristic is that these baby boomers on the cultural left come from affluent families. They are typically the sons and daughters of successful, upper-middle-class business and professional people. This has been verified by much research. Indeed, their orientation toward self-fulfillment and inner direction is predicated on a level of affluence that satisfies basic needs and necessities so that other possibilities for the self are not only stimulated but move within the orbit of realization. Arnold Mitchell, for one, makes the case that a certain level of affluence is necessary for this kind of lifestyle to emerge.[1]

With this affluence came a third characteristic, a deep and abiding commitment to personal freedom and tolerance. "Doing one's own thing" was only one of the expressions that represented this extraordinary shift in U.S. lifestyles, but it communicated a deep commitment of the cultural left. This personal freedom became increasingly visible to the wider culture not only in personal dress and hairstyles but in new patterns of sexuality, nonfamily household arrangements, the women's movement, pro-choice on abortion, and gay and lesbian lifestyles. Hence, the personal freedom was accompanied by a high tolerance for diverse behaviors and pluralistic opinions. This tolerance meant that other persons were free to pursue their individual wishes as long as these did not infringe on one's own freedom. Personal freedom and tolerance of this kind would draw angry responses from others in the society, especially from many on the cultural right who excoriated what they saw as relativism, amoral and immoral proclivities, and a corruption of family values predominant on the cultural left.

Much of the political activity of the new right and the new Christian right cannot be adequately understood apart from this reaction against the cultural left, which ignited their sense that someone had indeed changed the rules from the traditional values and conventional morality they had taken for granted until the late 60's and early 70's.

Among the U.S. Americans on the cultural left can be found quite distinct subgroups or lifestyle variations. While each of these is characterized by self-fulfillment, inner direction, and an intense commitment to toleration and personal freedom, certain distinctive groups can nevertheless be found. I want to address three of these, and I am here especially indebted to the work of Arnold Mitchell.[2]

The first group Mitchell describes as I-am-mes. This is a transition stage that usually lasts only a few years. Ninety-one percent of them are under twenty-five years of age, and hardly any are over thirty. Usually reared in affluent circumstances by parents who were outer-directed achievers, they shift into "the evanescent, fanciful, mercurial, flighty styles of I-am-me peers and contemporaries." Theirs is a shift from the outer direction of their parents to new concerns and the psychic benefits of inner direction that alter the purposes and goals of their lives. This is the far deeper importance of their transition than the hairdos, clothing, conduct, and surly demeanor that are so much more visible.

Two friends of mine in their early forties took their daughter to Tulane University for her enrollment there. While on campus they attended the dean's reception. Their daughter, an attractive young woman, was soon approached by a young man who introduced himself as a Tulane football player (surely an oxymoron if there ever was one). He had rich, lush hair on his head and face, but with two unique features. First, his hair and beard were bright lavender in color, and, second, he indeed did have rich thick hair on one half of his head and face, but the other side was, Kojak-like, completely clean-shaven. My two friends stepped away to watch the conversation between the two young adults at a short distance. Whispering quietly, the wife asked her husband, "Dear, were we ever like that?"

"Oh, only for about a decade, I think," was his answer.

While it is a transitional state, so far the shift from outer direction to inner direction has continued. The I-am-mes of ten years ago or more seem to have held on to their new values. Meanwhile, the I-am-mes of today seem less extreme than their countercultural predecessors in the past. Today's I-am-mes have an abundance of energy, the daring of youth, an insistent appetite for the new, and an enthusiastic pursuit of a broad range of social, cultural, and intellectual activities and physically challenging sports. They do not, however, seem to have spent much time on the social issues currently facing the nation.

The second inner-directed group on the cultural left is the Experientials, a group committed to immediate, vital experience. They have a yearning for deep personal involvement and hands-on engagement with life. For some it is with ideas or issues, but for others it may take on a hedonistic expression, or the demands of hard physical exploits such as rock climbing and backpacking. For still others the call to inner exploration is most compelling. With a few the call to a lifestyle of voluntary simplicity is central to their lives. Theirs is a lifestyle that loves noise and excitement but also seeks out the mystical through focusing on the interiority of the self, its thoughts, emotions, and spirit life. They crave authenticity, turn away from repressed feeling, ignore the façades of formality, tend to distrust established institutions and authority, and seek to relate to things intuitively.

Independent, self-reliant, mostly in their late twenties, they are well educated, with incomes above the national average. Experientials tend to be happy, psychologically healthy people who are confident and self-assured. With a tendency to be politically liberal, they support the women's movement, reductions in military spending, sex outside marriage, the legalization of marijuana, and ecological and consumer movements.

Most Experientials have a decided preference for the natural and are convinced of the essential rightness of nature. Therefore they believe in holistic medicine and natural foods and seek out opportunities to commune with nature.

Finally, while they are drawn to mystical experience, they do not seek it in Western religions for the most part and especially not in organized religion. Their own personal insights and views are more important, although these may be informed by Zen, Yoga, martial arts, Tao Te Ching, or other Eastern approaches. For others, a path to self-discovery and the mystical is sought through transcendental meditation, self-hypnosis, or disciplined introspection. Of course, some seek inner illumination or escape through the wide range of drugs so abundantly available in our society.

The third group on the cultural left is the Societally Conscious, a lifestyle represented by some 14 million Americans who are deeply concerned about social issues. Conservation, consumer matters, environmental integrity, social justice, and peace issues are among the key interests of this group. Some are politically assertive, even aggressive, and others work in a more moderate style through networks to achieve change. Still others seek out a life of "living simply that others may simply live."

This group shares some basic convictions. They believe in the integrity of nature, that it is not to be dominated but cooperated with, that it has a wisdom of its own, that the world really is one, and that in a materialistic society the nonmaterial dimensions of living are richer and more meaningful. They are pronature and postmaterialist. While only a few of them live lives of genuine simplicity, nevertheless they often drive economy cars, use solar energy, insulate their homes, and consume foods grown without pesticides and additives.

Politically sagacious and cosmopolitan, they have an average age of just under forty. A whopping 39 percent have graduate school education, and 59 percent are in professional or technical jobs. Next to Achievers they have the highest level of income of all of Mitchell's nine lifestyles.

While they constitute only 8 or 9 percent of the adult population, their numbers are increasing rapidly, and they have a disproportionate effect on society because they, more than anyone else, have made use of "single-issue politics." This tactic allows relatively small numbers of the Societally Conscious to block and frustrate concerns and goals to which much larger numbers of people are committed. Their confrontational style can be seen in someone like Ralph Nader. "The overall picture is of a well-educated, prosperous, politically liberal group driven by social ideals that they take with high seriousness."[3]

The New Age Movement

Found among the three groups on the cultural left—and in the cultural middle, for that matter—is a group known as New Agers. Affluent baby boomers are the group most attracted to the New Age movement, which includes a broad range of activities from the occult to the conventional such as health food, channeling, astrology, crystals, mind/body awareness, visits to past lives, environmental protection, meditation, acupuncture, spiritual healing, ethical investing, and so on. At least two very broad groups are discernible. One of these would agree with the editors of *New Age Journal,* who see themselves attempting "to carve out the credible end of New Age thinking." They appeal to affluent, educated, widely traveled, urban sophisticates who are searching for something quite different from the usual offerings of American society. They seek, rather, transformative alternatives, holistic personal life, and new paradigms or frameworks for interpreting and acting in the world. Some want enlightenment through interior journeys; others pursue utopia.[4]

The second and more popular group, however, seems to get the most attention. Self-styled past-life journeyer Shirley McLaine probably comes first to mind. Her 1983 autobiography *Out on a Limb* has 4 million copies in print, suggesting the confidence that Bantam Books, her publisher, has in its salability. Bantam editor Leslie Meredith contends that the New Age reader is a person who wants "self-fulfillment and, beyond that, a better community and world."[5] Yet many of the core group of New Agers contend that too much hocus-pocus trivializes the more serious concerns of those baby boomers who have abiding involvements in spirituality and social change. Serious New Agers are about 7 percent of the adult population of the United States, or about 11.7 million people, according to Jay Ogilvy, now with the Esalen Institute and formerly with Stanford Research Institute's Value and Lifestyles (SRI-VALS) program. With the growing popularity of the New Age movement, he estimates that many more Americans are now in the movement, though their participation has significantly watered down the movement philosophically.[6]

The New Agers are a part of the trend-setting group in the United States, explains John Garret of the SRI-VALS program. They are inner-directed and concentrated in the first wave of baby boomers. Not so materialistic in orientation, they want to experience life firsthand in ways that are exciting, rich, and full. The New Agers have little interest in organized religion; rather, they seek new religious forms that will provide an attunement to the world, a sense of unity, and a deeply interior communion with self, others, and cosmos.[7]

Ted Peters, a systematic theologian at Pacific Lutheran Theological Seminary, has provided an eightfold "common core of teachings" of New Age thought. What follows is my summary of these teachings.

1. *Holism.* An attempt to reintegrate body and spirit, self and community, society and nature, its individual and global ideas are "unity, peace, and harmony."
2. *A holism that is "metaphysical and mystical."* This is not merely a psychological or subjective principle but rather an ecstatic experience in one's own being of the cosmic unity of all being.
3. *The higher transpersonal self.* A self is sought beyond everyday experience that makes us one with other selves in a mystical realm. From time to time this self crashes into our ordinary consciousness, an event experienced as inspirational and characterized by an explosion of creativity and an energizing dynamic of healing. New Age methods of consciousness-raising seek entrée into a closer relationship with this higher self.
4. *Self-help.* This is a key concern because the enormous potential within each person awaits the use of a wide repertoire of educational, psychological, and spiritual techniques to change one's life circumstances radically toward the aims of self-fulfillment and self-realization.
5. *Reincarnation.* A significant teaching in New Age thought is the idea that the soul travels from one body to another through death and rebirth. It has led to reincarnation therapy, which uses hypnotism to take a person back into previous lives to points of bad decisions that led to bad karma. A catharsis at this point reverses, heals, and transforms the karma.
6. *Evolution and transformation.* The very name "New Age" connotes the sense that we are on the edge of some new dawning in the world. The term "evolution" is infused with the notion of progress. A transformation is in the offing wherein personal, psychological growth can be united with global harmony and fulfillment, based on cooperation, not competition, and where personal well-being and peace on earth are one in some evolutionary, paradigmatic shift standing now at the threshold of history and nature.
7. *Consciousness-raising.* A new understanding brought about through consciousness-raising is a central means of transformation. Such understanding is not usually found in scientific method as typically used; rather, it is keenly personal knowledge with such *saving* power that spiritual change can be wrought through it. This view understands divinity to be residing in our depths, a divinity that can be surfaced into our phenomenal selves to explore the potential for personal and world transformation and fulfillment.
8. *Jesus and cosmic consciousness.* Jesus is an important figure in much New Age thought and teaching. He is seen as "the prototypical expression of universal cosmic consciousness," one who, like Buddha, responded to the opportunity to go beyond the boundaries of the ordinary self and realize the divinity within and to become one with the all-encompassing source of cosmic and divine energy.[8]

Obviously, not all New Age people would agree with these eight points, and certainly not as so briefly sketched. My purpose in this summary is rather to provide church persons with some sense of how different New Age views are from those found in most churches. The gulf between the two is a broad sea.

I remember once teaching a course on social change in which we surveyed the thought of Karl Marx, Max Weber, and Émile Durkheim, three central figures in the classic tradition of Western sociology. I then asked the students to prepare a paper on doing social change as informed by the analyses of these three great social theorists. One woman in the class whom I knew to be deeply committed to New Age thought turned in a paper that mentioned absolutely nothing we had talked about or read for the course. The paper was well written and reflected many of the eight points of Peters's "common core of teachings." The paper was obviously done with much care and thought but quite simply did not fulfill the assignment.

When I asked the student to talk with me in my office and confronted her with my concern, she said, "Look, Tex, I can tell you all that stuff about Marx, Weber, and Durkheim. Do you want to hear it?"

"Not yet," was my tentative reply.

"Well," she said, "all of that is just traditional scholarship. It is simply out of touch with the personal, social, and cosmic transformation that is already under way. Tex, your problem is that you are mired in the nineteenth and twentieth centuries and you need to open yourself to a new dawning of consciousness that is occurring all over the world."

One can see why it may be difficult for people in the church to communicate with New Age people, and it does not take much imagination to see that New Age thought represents a major challenge to mainline churches. I doubt that the differences between this precocious student and me are much different from those of most church leaders and New Age devotees on the cultural left.

In summary, the cultural left is made up of a group of about 33 million Americans, mostly baby boomers who seek self-fulfillment while being inner directed and marching to their own drum. Moreover, the cultural left is composed of three basic lifestyles: The I-am-mes, the Experientials, and the Societally Conscious. In the midst of the cultural left is also a large group of New Age devotees.

The people in our society who are least likely to attend church are those on the cultural left. While many surveys report that even the cultural left confesses belief in God, Christ, life after death, and so on, these are "believers without belonging" in Carl Dudley's phrase.[9] They, along with many cohorts of their age in the cultural middle, are the basic reason for the decline of mainline churches.[10]

If the church is to reach this sizable group of baby boomers, it simply cannot do business as usual. These folk believe quite clearly that one does not have to go to church to be a good Christian. With their inner direction, they will not respond to shoulds, oughts, obligations, or appeals for long-term commitments. One baby boomer, told by his father that he should go to church, reacted immediately: "Dad, don't should on yourself!"

Is there anything the church can do? Can self-denial churches draw self-fulfillment baby boomers? This is the concern of the next chapter.

▶3◀

Strategy for Reaching the Cultural Left

The cultural left represents a major challenge to the churches. Clearly, they are the most difficult people to reach by traditional church worship, program, and outreach. Moreover, in spite of the recent increased return of baby boomers to church, the cultural left is least likely to participate in this shift, so that the churches will have to take new steps in order to attract these boomers who are the most distant from organized religion.

The task of this chapter is to outline the direction the church needs to go in order to reach the cultural left more effectively. Such a direction must take seriously the lifestyle differences and must rethink the approaches of the church in light of these differences.

Program Guidelines

The first step is to develop guidelines for the church. These are criteria, if you will, for evaluating the effectiveness of an idea or proposal. The first of these is that the program needs to be intrinsically valuable—it needs to be worthwhile in and of itself. Cultural-left people will not go to church out of obligation, and they certainly won't go if they know that an event is going to be dull and of low quality. Warren Hartman has suggested that programs for baby boomers need to be "complex, high quality programs that provide instant gratification and are user friendly."[1]

Second, it is important that programs be emotionally expressive. Cultural-left baby boomers simply will not go, out of obligation, to events they find boring. Like it or not, a careful reappraisal of worship, church school, and other events needs to be made. This is not to say that every church program has to be a feeling-charged orgy. Rather, the accommodation of mainline churches to a middle-class "thinking and doing" approach to religious life has tended toward formality, under-statement, modulated tones, and a week-in-week-out rehearsal of monotonous prose written for another time and another place.[2] Yet this kind of middle-class expression is often seen by its devotees as authentic, since they do not realize how culturally and class conditioned it is.

What I *do* mean is that an event such as worship requires movement, language that speaks to the world in which people live, that is not sicklied over with the esoteric lingo of some "liturgical experts," that touches because it is genuine, that names the experiences people have with God. God did not stop inspiring music after Bach, Beethoven, and Mozart, and contemporary music—yes, rock, jazz, blues, country, and so forth—has important contributions to make. Alternative worship experiences, perhaps not on Sunday morning, perhaps not using a sermon, need careful consideration. Such services could take greater advantage of silence, speak to the mystical, the therapeutic, the socially visioned dimension of people's lives—indeed, aim at a transformative event where God's grace is experienced in community and God's reign calls cultural-left boomers to new commitments.

A third guideline—and a very important one—is that programs focus on building deep and lasting relationships. Those churches that have been effective with baby boomers thus far have focused especially on the fact that baby boomers are relationally hungry. This is particularly true for the culturally left and means a rich community group life with a lot of options: worship, study, recreation, social activities, social action, spiritual formation, community service, and so on. Lyle Schaller has said that a church needs at least six or seven fellowship groups for every hundred members. Some such ratio as this is needed for cultural-left baby boomers.[3]

A fourth guideline is one that fits directly into the mission of the church. A large group on the cultural left, some 14 million according to Mitchell, are the Societally Conscious.[4] A church that wants to appeal to this group will have strong community outreach opportunities and active groups concerned about issues such as liberation, social justice, and ecological protection. Obviously, not everyone will be concerned about the same issues; therefore, it will be necessary, again, to provide options. When attempting to reach Experientials, remember that they simply may not stay with one issue but want to work on a variety of them. That a significant number of cultural-left baby boomers care about a range of issues central to the mission of the church is one of those occasions when the church's evangelical function in terms of proclaiming and witnessing to the gospel, its institutional need for membership recruitment, and its responsibility to do justice and service come together. On so many occasions the mission and the maintenance of the church are in conflict. It is a welcome coincidence when they are not.

In this connection it is important to know that cultural-left baby boomers are attracted to specific hands-on tasks in social service and justice ministries. Their interest in direct experience is evident here, plus their distrust of institutional efforts on the whole. Hands-on experience provides the experiential excitement most seek as well as offering the opportunity to do work that is credible because they are doing it. If neither of these results is forthcoming, the task is not likely to sustain their interest.

Fifth, baby boomers of the cultural left, and the middle for that matter, thus far have not typically been willing to make long-term commitments. This means that programming will focus on events, activities, and actions that are short-term. The cultural left will not commit itself to an ongoing program such as a church school class that meets every Sunday morning; rather, they are much more likely to agree to an event that meets once a week for three to six weeks. Hence, a Bible study of a certain duration, or a commitment to work on a specific piece of legislation during one legislative session, is more thinkable.

Finally, the diversity of the baby boomers needs to be kept in mind. As we have seen, they should not be stereotyped. This is also true for those on the cultural left. Some are single and single again; others are married, and some of these have children. Yet others live in households together but are not married and may have children. They will be different in yet other ways: Some are affluent, while many others struggle under stringent living conditions and so on. This diversity requires the complex group life opportunities already suggested, but it is important at all times to keep reminding oneself of the differences. Such an awareness not only avoids destructive stereotyping, it opens up new directions for strategy and programming.

Moreover, with all the cultural left's interest in mysticism, Eastern religion, New Age thought, and so on, it would be a mistake to see them all as hostile to the church. Surveys of the American people suggest that an overwhelming majority continue to have faith. Many of them also believe that the church is an important institution. But so far most of the cultural left has not found the church meeting their needs. As they so often say, "There's just nothing there for me." This attitude is not hostile. Thus, there is no reason for a church to despair of reaching the cultural left if that church has attempted to understand them, to be open to their concerns, and to have made an active effort to reach them.

With these guidelines in mind, we can now turn to the development of more concrete strategies for reaching the cultural left. These strategies will obviously not be exhaustive. They are meant to be suggestive, to initiate further thought and ideas, and to set a tone for action. If anything, they are meant to be a way to get started.

A Strategy for Reaching Baby Boomers

They very first step in a strategy to reach cultural-left baby boomers is to be sure that they are in the community around the church. Some years ago I studied a church that complained vigorously about their lack of young adults. They felt guilty that 80 percent of their congregation was over fifty years of age. While they had a vibrant ministry and mission, they felt endlessly plagued by the age of the congregation. When we reviewed the census tracts of the area, however, we found very few young adults. The people of that part of town *were* over fifty. The church reflected its community!

This will not be true of most churches, however, in that it is more likely that churches will not have a representative proportion of cultural-left baby boomers who are in their community. Nevertheless, some survey of the community to discover who *is* there is crucial, and the focus here is on churches in communities that do have baby boomers but have not been able to reach them.

Many churches are aging rapidly and yet find themselves in communities full of young adults. Where this is true, the future of a church usually hangs on its ability to reach these young adults. One of the truisms of church studies is that once a congregation loses its relationship to the community around it, it is only a matter of time before that church dies. Reaching the cultural left, then, becomes a fateful challenge to such churches.

The lifestyles of baby boomers on the cultural left and middle will pose problems for many church members. The self-fulfillment orientation, their difficulties in making long-term commitments, their consumer orientation to church life, their liberality on social issues such as sexuality and morality, the strange view of New Age thought, and so on will put off more traditional church members. As a result it will be necessary to give significant legitimation to efforts to reach them and to programs that prove effective.

The most powerful legitimative rationale I have found with most church people is to ask how many of their adult sons and daughters are active in the church. When the hands go up in the room, there are only a small minority every time. I then ask what they would be willing for churches to do in the communities where their offspring live in order to get them involved in the life of the church. I have found astounding commitment because these older church members carry tremendous guilt about their adult children's failure to relate to the church. While I do not think the parents are guilty, they themselves do. They really want to see their sons and daughters back in the church. When the question is raised this way, I seldom find significant resistance to making genuine outreach attempts with boomers of the cultural left and middle.

At the same time it is important to remember that those in the church now will continue to need ministry and support. It would be an awful mistake to ignore the congregation that has been there all along. By keeping faith with these relationships, the continuity of the church is sustained. A pastor or a church leader simply must not convey to those who have been faithful people across the years that they are no longer a priority. Such a strategic blunder can have lethal consequences for the effectiveness of church leadership.

When a church has a small group of baby boomers, it is helpful to plan to meet with them. A personal invitation, followed by a phone call explaining the purpose of the meeting, will secure a better turnout. At the meeting it needs to be explained—briefly—what has been going on in the wider society and why the church wants to offer ministry to their generation. Then the session can turn to one of planning future pro- grams, group meetings, and so on in which they have genuine interest. I find it very important not to plan *for* baby boomers but to plan *with* them.

One should expect these boomers to make plans that do not fit in with the present program and schedule of the church, and here the attitude of the pastor and others working with them is paramount. If one seems closed, uptight about new ideas, and overly cautious or heavy- handed about decisions, the difficulties of reaching baby boomers become intense indeed. Martha Farnsworth Riche was asked in a con- sultation if people who were older than baby boomers could work effectively with them. She answered in the affirmative and added that what is important is the attitude and the openness of those who seek to do so.[5]

Robert Gribbon of the Alban Institute has provided a helpful refinement of the leadership styles needed by baby boomers at different age levels. He observes that those who are eighteen to twenty-five years old need a friend; those twenty-five to thirty appreciate a mentor, someone who can provide savvy and guidance; and those over thirty seem most of all to want a co-worker.[6]

Let me add one word of caution about beginning with the baby boomers already active in the church. They are more likely to be cul- turally right and right of center. While it is important to reach these people, they will often not be able to attract those of the cultural left, especially, and even those on the left of center. Those on the left will quite likely have to be touched in other ways. Still, one must begin somewhere, and beginning with baby boomers already related to the church is useful because it provides a way to do some careful planning with them, to experiment with new ideas, to experience a few failures that one hopes the church can sustain, and to enjoy some successes that build relationships among those involved.

After a plan has been developed, some care needs to be exercised in taking the plan before the board of the church. I once worked through two three-hour sessions with a group of twenty boomers who did an excellent job of planning a program for the next three months. It involved an alternative worship service, some social activities that were unconventional but not really way out, and some requests for staff support. When the pastor took it to the board, they laughed and turned the proposal down cold.

It just so happened that a physician in his fifties had participated as a lay leader in the planning with the group but had to miss the board meeting. When he heard what had happened, he got word to the boomer group that he would take the plan back to a special meeting of the board and hoped they would not become discouraged until he had tried again. When he went to the board, he shared in some detail how important the effort was and explained the necessity of such moves. His standing in the church and his persuasiveness resulted in a very strong approval of the plan. Had the possibility of board disapproval been anticipated before the first meeting and a careful presentation been thought through, the plan quite likely would have not had the initial reversal.

To reach cultural-left people outside the church, several steps are necessary. A first one is to study the points of entry into the church that baby boomers have taken in the recent past. Often this is the church's music program. If several groups have been effective, these efforts need to be named and extended. A choir, for example, may be the best access point. Choir members can be actively encouraged to invite others. An enthusiastic invitation with an offer to help break the ice in the new group has proved to be key for many people. At the same time, it may be more helpful to begin a new choir or choral group with an alternative type of music or style of approach. Then new people have the chance to get in on the formation of the group and its development. Studies have shown that baby boomers appreciate opportunities like this. For example, some cultural-left baby boomers have taken very active roles in the beginning of new churches.

A second way to involve those outside the church is through advertising. For a long time I had little confidence in such approaches, yet research on the boomers, including the cultural left, suggests that they can be reached by advertising of a certain kind. Boomers are an information-oriented group but may not respond to advertisements in general. Rather, the information should be quite specific and concrete in terms of what is offered. The claims must be credible, and the church that makes them needs to be able to back them up. Hence, a mailing or an advertisement in the media that is specific, concrete, and explicitly aimed at the cultural left will have the best chance of reaching them.

Third, because of the diverse interests of the baby boomers those churches that offer option-filled programs and alternative approaches to traditional church life will attract more people on the cultural left. Their mystical-therapeutic interests, their hopes of combining spirituality and social transformation, their experimental approach to life as a buffet, their recreational and social needs, their concern for quality religious education for their children, their hunger for relationships and ongoing quest for identity—all of these suggest that churches with a highly advertised array of offerings make the most strategic outreach to the cultural left.

Any strategy for reaching the cultural left requires recognition of how busy they are. They have the highest proportion of their generation working outside the home for pay in the history of the United States. If we can trust the data now coming in, most of them are under serious financial constraints. With the overwhelming majority it is not because they overspend nearly so much as because they underearn.[7]

A strategic response by the church that recognizes the press of their schedules and the stress of their personal lives as well as their social-religious interests can be a genuine ministry to the cultural left. When asked about what they would like to do most if they had more free time, the number-one answer is "sleep." With lives like these, the church cannot do business as usual. Moreover, with the huge increase of women working outside the home for pay, the church cannot depend on the enormous volunteer role once played by women.

Church programming, then, with the cultural left begins by look-ing for niches in their lives where the church can offer a ministry that provides an intrinsically valuable experience of worship, one that is emotionally expressive, that opens up the opportunity for new relation-ships, and that can deliver, out of this, occasions for short-term, hands-on servant ministry to the world.

For example, a church could offer a late-afternoon, after-work catered meal with healthful food at below fast-food prices. Child care would be provided. Holy Communion, with a brief ritual and no homily, would be part of the meal. The entire event would last no more than forty-five minutes for those who need to leave and could even be shorter. For those who wished to follow the meal with options in music, study, reflection and action on issues, recreation, social time, and so forth, such opportunities could be provided. A program like this assures the Eucharist every week, eliminates the need for participants to prepare supper, supplies child care, gives occasion for developing new relation-ships, has additional options after the meal if desired, and fits into a time in their lives that could reduce the hectic pressure of the supper hour immediately after work. Those who wanted to go home immediately would be home by six thirty or so and have the entire evening ahead of them. While this would not be the answer everywhere, such a program demonstrates the kind of thinking and planning necessary to reach highly scheduled cultural-left people.

In their struggles with relationships and commitment, baby boomers can be approached from yet another angle. Many of them are highly mobile geographically. For this reason they are not near parents and other family. Others, in part because of lifestyle issues, may be estranged from parents and family. As a result the church can be "absentee kin," says Warren Hartman, who maintains that the church can provide "stability and a sense of connectedness." In his study of churches doing effective work with baby boomers, he found that the older members in some churches become both surrogate parents and faith mentors. The "old saints" of the church can serve as guides, as steady and sturdy examples and witnesses of what a lifetime of journey in the faith can mean. Moreover, the church through its rituals can provide opportunity for the cultural left and middle to experience bonding and connectedness. Hartman reported on one church where the pastor encouraged baby-boomer parents to invite all their relatives and friends to the baptisms of infants so that the event could take place in the rich relational context of family, friends, and congregation. Such rituals create and deepen bonding, opening the way to healing community and empowering commitment.[8]

Karen Greenwaldt has suggested an approach that uses a party motif. She points out that celebration, community, fun, and compassion can all go together. In the church where she is a member and works as a volunteer with young adults, they have used a party as the occasion for dealing with a wide range of interests and concerns. In one case, the church learned that there was a serious shortage of shoes for homeless people in the city of Nashville, so they threw a well-advertised shoe party. It *was* a party, but entrance to the occasion could be gained only by bringing a pair of shoes for the homeless. Not only did they have a huge turnout, but many people came by who could not attend but wanted to drop off a pair of shoes. As a result they collected enough shoes for the next year and a half. They also had voter registration parties and a tax party on April 15 where the place mats were IRS forms.[9]

I can imagine a party on environmental protection. The room or rooms could be turned into a learning center on ecological issues. Participants could be encouraged to build displays on deforestation, desertification, environmental pollution, ozone depletion, the salinization and alkalinization of soil, nuclear wastes, toxics, the adulteration of food, and so on. Action groups in the area could be invited to give direction for further reflection and action. This party motif can be used in many ways and coheres well with many lifestyle attributes of baby boomers. A party has the advantage of being a one-time event and hence is short term, but the party motif makes it possible to have continuing events and ongoing relationships. More than that, parties can be intrinsically worthwhile, emotionally expressive, community building, and focused on social concerns.

The cultural left also has special needs in terms of type of household or family. Many of the baby boomers have children, often only one, but these parents are looking for quality religious instruction for their children and often for themselves. Programs that interrelate and coordinate for children, youth, and parents reinforce family efforts to make church a part of their lives. These programs include corporate worship, church school, weekday preschool, support groups for new mothers, parenting classes, a variety of musical groups, prayer, study opportunities, exercise groups, parents' day out, Bible study, and so on. Any or all of these can be accompanied by child care and other groups for children and youth. Lyle Schaller has pointed out how important the nursery is for these young parents. A deep, dark dungeon of a nursery that smells like moldy old church-school literature is hardly an asset but an outright detriment to a church's capacity to attract them.[10]

Singles are another key group, including those who are single again. There are in fact 19 million people who live alone in the United States, and they constitute a major opportunity for the church to do ministry. A broad range of groups with sufficient complexity to meet the diverse and specialized interests of singles is required if the church is to respond. Again, such groups can focus on matters such as support, social activities, recreation, study, prayer, spirituality, and sports.

Nothing said so far should imply that the cultural left will not be drawn to explicitly religious programs aimed at deeply felt spiritual needs. The will to completion in God, the appetite for meaningful life, the searching out of the strange ways in which the Spirit seems alternately to challenge us and lure us—these are not absent in the cultural left. If some have turned toward Eastern religion or popular technologies of the soul, it is not because of a failure of interest in the life of the spirit but a sense that the church is not the place to find it. As they grow older, many will look again to their roots, if they had them, to see if there may yet be answers in the church. Others who never had a church experience may look toward mainline congregations that don't offer mindless simplisms, uncivil fundamentalism, happiness cults, fatuous solutions, or heretical perversions of the gospel of wealth.

Pastors now report that there are cultural-left and other baby boomers who are utterly ignorant of the Bible but who have a compelling desire to study it. Others observe that the recent work of the church in spiritual formation speaks to the boomers. Pastors and others who can serve as spiritual guides discover a highly motivated group of journeyers. Some of these are burned out on the claims of pretentious supernaturalism of pop New Age thought. Still others have run headlong into deep trauma and tragedy and feel bereft by the naïveté of the affluent adaptations of the religious fads and fashions of the last twenty years. Yet still others have now reached a time of searching.

They will not be helped much by middle-class accommodative and domesticated cultural Christianity, yet there is in the tradition's deepest and most faithful currents a tide of power adequate to this or any age. A church that openly acknowledges the mystery of God, that despairs of empty formulas and overwrought propositional truth, that welcomes strangers and other aliens as co-travelers on the way, and that faithfully and humbly claims Christ as Savior and Lord can be an authentic place to go to worship, learn, pray, and study, and from which to scatter to live, seek justice, make peace, and dream toward the transformation that God is bringing.

What does seem to be key at this point with baby boomers is their desire to discover the ways that faith can be specific and down to earth and can help them make it through the next week. For example, they do not tend to care what a particular denomination thinks about a given issue; they are more concerned about what the Bible has to say to them and how it can give pragmatic guidance for living in the workaday world.[11]

A Theological Reflection

When I have made proposals such as these to people in the churches, I am usually asked certain questions: "Are you selling out the gospel to a group of spoiled, immature young adults who need to grow up?" "Is this not simply the accommodation of the gospel to the lifestyles of contemporary life? What about the prophetic word of God?" "You are promoting a cultural Christianity. What expectations ought these people meet when they come into the church? Shouldn't they have to change?" These are important questions and are almost always sincerely asked. They deserve a response.

At the outset we need to recognize that *any* different lifestyle is always a problem for the church, not only that of the baby boomers on the cultural left. The tendency to accommodate Christ to a culture is pervasive in church history. Sallman's head of Christ turned Jesus into an Anglo with movie-star looks. Bruce Barton's *The Man Nobody Knows* made Jesus a Rotarian. The gospel of wealth makes him the greatest capitalist and speculator that ever lived. Those on the political left make him a revolutionary, and the pious make him a paragon of syrupy devotionalism. Those in self-denial lifestyles make him into an effective agent of repressing the self for the sake of respectability. The New Age makes him a channeler, a guru, or a guide. Athletes turn him into a jock, and rock lovers proclaim him a superstar. Churches make him a Roman Catholic, a Methodist, a Baptist, or a Disciple, and patriots make him American or English, a Pole, a Russian, or a Japanese.

So the questions are important—so important that they must be raised of every cultural formation. Such criticism, however, is most becoming when it begins in self-criticism. So let me be clear about three things. The first is that the gospel begins with people where they are. It does not stop there, with anyone. We confront a generation in the United States, at least great parts of it, who are unchurched. We simply cannot lay expectations on cultural-left baby boomers and anticipate a positive response. God accepts people as they are: "Just as I am, without one plea." It is not far off the mark to propose that the church do so as well.

Second, it was Paul who maintained to the church at Corinth that he had been all things to all people (see 1 Cor. 9:22). His plan here was not one of accommodating the church to the various cultural arrangements he found. Rather, he said in another context that we are not in the world to conform to it but to transform it by the renewal of our minds (see Rom. 12:2). To be all things to all people is only a first step in this transformation.

Third, I will not propose here or anywhere, I hope, an unthinking, even if enthusiastic, identification of Christ with any culture or subculture. At the same time, no cultural formation can keep out the liberating and redeeming activity of the Spirit of Christ. At the end of Mark's Gospel the young man in bright clothing at the tomb told the disciples not to seek Jesus among the dead but the living and proclaimed that Jesus had stolen the march on them and had already preceded them to Galilee, where they would find him (see Mark 16:5–8). The task of the church is like that. We do not take Christ *any*where finally. This is not our problem. The challenge, rather, is to get ourselves there and to discover where the Spirit of Christ is at work; that is, find where the liberating and saving currents are and join in. So the position here is not one of the Christ of culture but the Christ *in* culture. The task of the church is to search out the presence and the work of the Spirit of Christ in the midst of the cultural left. One can be confident that Christ is already there.

Finally, people often object that baby boomers will not make commitments and that they should not be welcomed into the church until they are prepared to do so. It is true that baby boomers have had a hard time making lasting commitments. Again, this is a human problem, not only a baby-boomer one, but they do seem to have special difficulties here. Yet it simply does no good to tell people they ought to have commitments; interestingly enough, the Christian faith does not approach people this way, at least not in its authentic forms. According to the gospel God does not first require commitment. Instead, God acts in our behalf, sends Christ to live and die for us, and raises Christ as our promise and hope. Christian faith does not begin by telling us what *we* must do, but by proclaiming what God has already done. God first establishes a relationship through God's action. Only later when we trust and receive God's gift of grace in faith do we understand that true faith is active in love and justice and in acts of mercy and self-giving. At the very heart of the gospel is the dynamic in which relationship precedes commitment. Indeed, commitments that are rigorously pursued without relationship to God have an uncanny propensity to works righteousness.

So perhaps the church needs to approach the cultural left with gratitude and humility: gratitude to God for what has been done for us, and gratitude for redemptive activity among the baby boomers, and humility so that we do not presume some pedestal of favored status before God in comparison to them.

It is not enough, however, to accept cultural-left baby boomers where they are because the way they approach matters of religious faith is different from that of most other Americans. This is especially true for those on the cultural left. If one is to do theology effectively, a different metaphor will be required. Their social experience, their approaches to issues of mystery and meaning, are not the same as those who actively participate in established churches. This is the subject of the next chapter.

▶4◀

Journey Theology

As I address the question of "types" of theology in the three broad lifestyle groupings in this book, the focus will not be on doctrine and certainly not on systematic theology. Rather, the focus will be on the lifestyle context of the cultural left, middle, and right to discover the basic metaphors by which faith can be approached. The conviction here is that faith is always embedded in a context and that the doing of theology involves reflection on an action in the context. In so doing, a lifestyle is to be neither romanticized nor paternalized; it is to be understood in terms of the psychological, social, historical, and religious dimensions of its context.

Such an approach to theology recognizes that there is always tension between Christ and culture and that critical reflection is an ongoing responsibility. One must be especially sensitive to issues of oppression and domination and the role of the church and the gospel to be a liberative and transformative current within culture. This approach also maintains that God is already at work in any culture or lifestyle and that discerning God's action is basic to the doing of theology and the mission of the church.

Let us then turn to the basic metaphor of the cultural left. In many conversations over the years and in the wide assortment of reading I have done, one metaphor stands out sharply with respect to the cultural left. It seems to catch the special drift of their experience. In this chapter, therefore, we shall be looking at journey theology.

Journey Theology

Thirty-five years old and the son of a distinguished pastor in the United Methodist Church, he appeared before his denomination's Board of Ordained Ministry, the group assigned the responsibility of examin-

ing candidates for ministry before ordination and the preceding pro-
bationary period. After a satisfying conversation with this baby boomer,
who clearly had social and intellectual skills for ministry, one of the
pastors on the board asked a question he thought would lead to closure
of the interview.

"So, John, you feel called to ordained ministry?"

"Oh, yes, indeed, at this point in my life I feel quite clearly called.
It's very important."

"What do you mean by 'at this point' you feel called?"

"Well, just that. Right now, I feel called in my faith journey to go
into ministry."

"But, John, the call to ordained ministry is a lifelong commitment.
People don't have it and then lose it."

"Oh, but they do. I know many people who were called and served
for a time as very effective pastors. They later felt pulled in new directions. That's OK; that doesn't take away from their call at that time or
from the effective job they did."

"But God doesn't call you to something and suddenly drop it."

"I don't see why not. Why can't God do something if it's God's
will? Aren't we imposing limits on God by insisting that God always has
to do something one way?"

This conversation was the beginning of a long, hard debate in that
board about the nature of the call and ordination. It has not been
resolved. This true story illustrates an important aspect of the way baby
boomers approach faith, especially those on the cultural left. It is defin-
itely not restricted to those seeking ordination. It is a tendency of a great
many—the large majority, I estimate—who see spirituality as a journey.
Such language pops up frequently in their conversation and is an image
that informs the way they feel, think, evaluate, and approach faith.

Needless to say, the church, at least in its majority expressions,
does not know what to do with such people as John. They simply do not
fall conveniently in the ecclesiastical categories of most mainline
denominations. And, yet it is more than that. Many mainliners, not to
mention those in conservative churches, have serious questions of conscience about this worldview of baby boomers, with its emphasis on
individual expression, relativism, personal autonomy, and short-term
commitments.

Why is the metaphor of journey so important to baby boomers?
Jim Purdue, who is a spiritual life director in Iowa, suggests that it is
related to Toffler's idea in *Future Shock* that life is lived in modules,
meaning that we live our lives in different segments or stations and may
do different things at different degrees of maturity or quality or importance.[1] We do not grow evenly across the board; rather, we develop at
different degrees from one place to another. In Purdue's view the jour-

ney is the line that connects the modules and gives continuity because the modules themselves cannot.

Such an orientation surely emerges from the social conditions in which baby boomers were born and developed. Martha Farnsworth Riche observed that baby boomers do not live in a world where one can expect to live in the house where one was born. Neither can one buy a house and expect to live in it for the rest of one's life. Indeed, one cannot easily expect to live one's entire life with the same spouse. The increasing longevity of life itself has caused this alteration, not to mention the high rate of divorce and the vast lifestyle changes, some of which we have already discussed.[2]

It is not hard to see why a generation that prizes honesty would be so hesitant to make lifelong commitments or to make claims that seem to fly in the face of their experience. One's faith and one's understanding of it will be affected. In all fairness one must grant that there is considerable realism in this assessment of their circumstances. What, then, does this mean?

It means, first of all, that faith will be a process, not an arrival.[3] The word "journey" gives this a concrete kind of expression but also conveys a sense of adventure. It connotes new experience, surprise, and avoids the idea of being permanently in a rut. Moreover, the notion of journey involves struggle and hardship. Yet the fact that these occur within a journey—and thus with some understanding that these negative experiences can be passed through and eventually overcome—provides a sense of perspective and of hope.

Second, the notion of journey is a metaphor for growth, movement, and development. This growth is both external and internal. Moving through the modules of contemporary life is a journey that involves introspection and the search for a rich interiority. It is self-filling and self-fulfilling. For this reason many baby boomers will not consider creeds nearly as important as autobiography and spiritual or faith walks.

Third, the journey metaphor typically occurs along with a profound sense of the inter- and inner-connectedness of all things. The journey is a walk through a world, really a cosmos, that extends out—and in—on every side. The ecological interests of those of the cultural left, their yearning for naturalism, their belief in the coherent wholeness, finally, of all things, and their search for a world that combines thought *and* feeling, doing *and* being, willing *and* letting be and letting go—all these aspirations are dimensions of the interrelated unity of all things. This unity can be affirmed by the cultural left even in the midst of a world riveted by violence and living under catastrophic threat.

This sense of interconnected unity is related to a fourth aspect, the persistent mystical, therapeutic, and experimental character of the spirituality of baby boomers. This fourth aspect of journey hungers for the combining of the inner and outer, the visible and invisible world. It is holistic in the cosmic sense as well as in the psychological. It can be found presently in a more secular search for success that has both an inner and outer quality. The interest in Eastern religions, Native American culture, parapsychic and contemporary New Age spirituality, yoga and transcendental meditation—all these reflect this pervasive concern,[4] so pervasive indeed that the journeyer seeks in some way to discover that life is, finally, a unified cycle, where all the components come together.[5] Journey is that living, moving, experiencing, feeling, deepening, growing search by which the fragments are brought together.

The Social Conditions of Journey Theology

For a generation that is inner-directed, the continuity and stability of life are not found in conformity to established institutions and their continuation. As a result one does not "fit in" to those institutions. They are not home. Journey is not a residence in major institutions but seeks the horizon of an expressive individualism and an ever-receding cornucopia of possibilities awaiting realization.

For this reason journey offers hope and a freeing to some new vitality in life. I have been struck time and time again by how important it is to baby boomers to discover adequate ways to express feelings: "I just have to find a way to get my feelings out." Or, "I have such strong emotions, but I just can't find the way to express them."

Why is it that adequate expression of feeling is so difficult? Related to it, why the search for relationships, for self-fulfillment, for a sense of oneness? Indeed, why the kind of "me" orientation that nettles so many older U.S. Americans? I think it ties directly to the deep alienation many older baby boomers experienced in the Vietnam War and the civil rights movement. Both of these events brought into sharp focus the hypocrisies of our national life. They led to a deeper estrangement from core institutions than any previous generation. Not only government but the economy, the church, and others were severely questioned and distrusted. Beyond these, the norms about sexuality, marriage, family, commitments, and morality were challenged and in many instances radically changed, if not discarded.

To be alienated from such core social realities means that the connection between one's deepest feeling and the institutionalized framework of social life is broken.

For some this broken connection has a psychically numbing effect and a loss of the capacity to feel or, at least, to focus feelings. For most, however, it is rather a question of what to do with the feelings they have, including how to talk about them. In commenting on an earlier draft of the manuscript, Susan Ruach, a clergyperson, baby boomer, and student of these things, says that "our language is not very precise around feelings." We don't know "how to express them and what to do when the feelings . . . simply do not fit into scientific and rational categories and are therefore scary to a lot of folks." One should not miss in this comment the complaint about "scientific and rational categories" and the degree to which the central institutions of U.S. life are shaped by them. This disjunction between personal feeling and the rationalized, bureaucratic organization of government, business, education, religion, and just plain everyday lived reality is a common experience for the cultural left.

A human being is a socius with a personal center.[6] The socius is a complex range of relationships to institutions that form the personal, inward conversations one has. Institutions, relationships, and our experiences with them make up consciousness. For example, if I relate to someone I love, my behavior, my language—yes, even my emotions—are formed out of my social experience. While I have a centered self capable of making an object of myself and reflecting my thoughts, feelings, actions, and evaluations, nevertheless my social experience is the content, the forms, the very framework of my consciousness. One is a centered self, but one is also composed of social experience. To be alienated from core institutions, then, to see oneself as different from, to define oneself over against, is to lose relationships that are not only external but internal. The result is to lose the emotional charges of these relationships and to suffer a social and personal gulf between the self and the institutionalized framework of the wider society.

For example, when the United States entered World War II, I was six years old. I identified strongly with my country. Franklin Delano Roosevelt had ended the Depression; America was fighting Nazis in the west and the perpetrators of Pearl Harbor in the east. On my garage wall I painted U.S. MARINE, and in my backyard I fought day after day the battles of Normandy and Bastogne, of Iwo Jima and Okinawa. The postwar years brought the Cold War and aroused my deep suspicions of the "godless Communists" and the Russian threat. High school in the early 50's was a time of jalopies, sock hops, dances, complexion problems, high school plays, sports, rock and roll, Hank Williams, and absolutely maddening crushes on girls who brought my hormones to a lather. I was a trumpet player and blew taps for those young men brought home from Korea in caskets. I chilled during the reading of their heroic sacrifices and shuddered as twenty-one-gun salutes crashed over the muffled weeping of their parents.

While I had reason later to be much more critical of my naïve and simplistic view of the world in the 40's and 50's, I never lost my feelings for those young men brought home in boxes. Yet the experience of baby boomers was radically different. For them the United States was involved in what is arguably the most questionable and immoral war of our country's history. The scientific, bureaucratic, technological character of that war with its weapons of destruction and its body counts, its daily entrance into our home via TV, and its destruction of a village in order "to save it" had a reality and a feel radically different from what I had known in the 40's. The civil rights movement threw into question assertions about the United States as a place "with liberty and justice for all." The assassinations of President Kennedy, Martin Luther King, Jr., and Robert Kennedy raised searching questions about the nation and convinced millions that we had indeed lost our way. The hypocrisy of what we said and what we did was not lost on baby boomers. The insularity of the great majority of our churches—"God's frozen people"—avoiding controversy and preaching privatistic, self-help psychologies of personal adjustment were just plain irrelevant, except for their complicity in a society shot through with moral contradiction.

The point is that baby boomers, especially on the cultural left, cannot be understood apart from this disjunction between their feelings and institutional life. Their lives have been profoundly conditioned by this socially pervasive estrangement and alienation.

To be sure, these experiences occurred in a time of unprecedented affluence, and it is easy to dismiss their moral objections as the frivolous dramatics of a generation unencumbered by the struggle for basic necessities, but such dismissal has to ignore mammoth fissures of injustice in the U.S. experience. That the critics were affluent does not diminish the acuity of the criticism.

It is likely that affluence provided the conditions for their inner direction, but the evils of Vietnam and racism severed their commitment to our institutions and tore apart the established patterns of cultural life.

To be sure, their responses were diverse. Some rebelled against the affluence as well and became, and remain, postmaterialists. A few became yuppies—4 to 6 percent, depending on where the income line for yuppiedom is drawn—and in an uncertain world bought into the affluence, determined to get theirs in order to live out the self-fulfillment their careers would provide. Most, however, were belted by the economic reversals of the 70's and continue to struggle financially, discovering that for most baby boomers two incomes are necessary to make it now. The 80's brought little relief for most boomers. The movement of entire companies and factories overseas, foreign competition, the buyouts of large corporations that did nothing for and in many cases hurt employees, the rising cost of education and increasing debt loads with student loans, the high price of housing and medical care, the low earnings of most baby boomers—all these and more have brought a greater "economic realism" (grimness may be the better word), but they have not healed the alienation between baby boomers and the institutions of our national life.

If anything, alienation and affluence, followed by economic stringency and a widely held view that their situation will be downwardly mobile compared to that of their parents, led all the more to an interpretation of life as journey. By what means can one possibly understand this flow of circumstances except as a journey? As some baby boomers still say, "It's a trip; it's a real trip."

It should not be surprising that commitment and relationships have been difficult for most baby boomers. To be inner-directed, alienated, defined generationally as a unit, and out of harmony with the conformist orientations of the 50's—these are more than enough to depreciate ongoing commitment and to throw one onto new ground where confusion reigns about the way relationships are formed and sustained.[7] It is not strange that life would be seen as journey or that it needs theological interpretation along the lines of this motif.

Such a motif is not unknown to the Christian faith and to a biblical understanding of the world. The Ark of the Covenant was carried along with the people. In the Exile the Jews knew what it was to be moved forcefully from their homeland, and in the New Testament the notion of being aliens was assumed in several writings, for example, Hebrews 11:13–16 and 1 Peter 1:17; 2:11. John Bunyan's *The Pilgrim's Progress*, among others, represented this view in church tradition.

With baby boomers, especially on the cultural left, the idea of journey does not mean that this is an alien *world*. While one may be on a journey, it is nevertheless a journey with a deep appreciation for nature, for the cosmos. It is a search for the connectedness of things. A strong hunger for establishing contact with the world and people is clear. If one's present setting is not home, the world is. Moreover, with baby boomers who are Societally Conscious in Mitchell's sense, care for the environment, for the world, is powerful. The popular song, "We are the world; we are the children," was not only a tremendous success in fund raising but struck deeply into the hearts of people, including baby boomers across the land. Closely related to this is Ray Charles's rendition of "America the Beautiful." The fact that it is sung by a black man who represents the victimization of a race with all its tragedy gives the song a new integrity from which a deep love of country and mystical appreciation for the land touch lost hungers to discover new ways to be an American and to applaud the awesome beauty of the continent. The massive national rituals in recent years to raise money for hunger, farm aid, and so on derive their appeal partly from the widely representative nature of the artists and the sense of the human unity of the planet.

These rituals are steps along the journey, but they depict a dream that can be placed on the horizon, a compelling vision of a humanity united in its compassion for others and its love for the world. They are significant expressions of the yearnings of many Americans and especially baby boomers.

In the midst of all this it should not be surprising that baby boomers have a profound love for their country. It is, however, an unrequited love, in their view. The magazine *Rolling Stone*, in a survey conducted by Peter Hart, found that a question about the heroes of these young adults led to the survey's most important disclosure. Their two most named heroes were Martin Luther King, Jr., and Robert Kennedy, both seen as larger than life in their idealism and yet both dead. These two figures stood for the values the generation still believes in, according to the survey: "peace and justice, tolerance and equality." Because no one in the past twenty years has taken up the mantle of these men, and because the evils they fought seem now even more intractable, theirs is a "blighted legacy." Ronald Reagan, quite popular in the early years of his administration, with his optimistic stress on the virtue and strength of America, deepened their disillusionment with government as a result of the scandals that smudged his image in the last two years of his administration.

Yet, there remains a smoldering, if suppressed, idealism. Having lost confidence in their capacity to change the world and having turned away from abstract moral causes, they remain committed to deal with the ordinary practical concerns of day-to-day life. And they long for *moral* leadership that possesses "the hard spiritual commandments" of a Dr. King and "the compassionate energy" of a Robert Kennedy. Presently, they wait.[8]

Their journey also has a mystical bent, and its naturalistic expressions have a strong therapeutic dimension. My colleague W. Paul Jones has been developing a framework of theological models he calls "theological worlds." In these he integrates Myers-Briggs personality types with basic theological orientations to the world, such as separation and reunion, conflict and vindication, emptiness and fulfillment, condemnation and forgiveness, and suffering and endurance. I have been struck over and over again by the utter fascination of baby-boomer students with these models. It is clear that this combination of psychotherapeutic types and theological worldviews has struck a poignantly vibrant chord of reality. Some students even suggest that it names something they have known for years without the capacity to frame it and claim its explanatory power. Such work as this by Jones offers a significant direction for doing theology.[9]

Journey Theology and New Age Thought

A theology that uses the metaphor of journey has a special relevance for conversation with New Agers. Indeed, much New Age thought uses the metaphor quite explicitly. More than that, New Age thought has contributions to make to the church in its attempt to *meet* many baby boomers on the cultural left.

Again, Ted Peters, in his discussion of the New Age movement, speaks appreciatively of its emphasis on holism and of its extensive use of psychological techniques and support groups, which he believes have affected positively "the emotional health of many people." Nevertheless, he is sharply critical of New Age teaching as naïve and unrealistic. He argues that "the God of Israel must be clearly distinguished from the world."[10] The world is a creation of God; it is not itself divine. I am troubled, however, that what begins in his critique as the need to *distinguish* God and the world results in a *separation* of God and the world with his reference to Kierkegaard's notion of the "infinite qualitative difference" between the creator and the creation. Such formulations seem to me to be clearly male and deserving of Mary Daly's wrath when she accuses such views as seeing God relating perpendicularly—that is, penis-wise—to the earth. A better view is one that distinguishes God and the creation yet sees God as the ultimate environment, the One in whom we live and move and have our being. Such a view, I believe, can make intelligible conversation with New Agers without making the now-known classic error of pantheism.

I do agree with Peters that there is a naïveté in New Age thought that to me makes it seem to float like an expensive, plaything bauble on a sea of economic exploitation, political domination, social alienation, existential estrangement, cultural hegemony, and historical futility. At the same time this is a world of magnificent beauty where relative justice does occur, where people can and do love, and where dreams of peace and the commonwealth of God burn deeply in the hearts and minds of so many. Such a mixed reality is not adequately understood by the positing of a God who is infinitely qualitatively different from the world, or by One who *is* the world.

The hard edges of evil will crash into the naïveté of the New Agers' thought. Yet their search for wholeness, for a transformative power at work in the world, is a deep longing in human experience, and there is no more powerful interpretive view of reality than that of the crucified God of Christian faith who holds the world "like a mammy bending over her baby,"[11] who is a God of love, liberation, and justice, and who can be met—as so often before—in the spiritual disciplines of the tradition. As the monks went to the "wilderness" to confront evil, as Julian of

Norwich broke through the categories of her time to stand ecstatically before the Motherhood of God, as dear Francis spoke to his brothers and sisters in nature, as Wesley sought sanctification and perfection, as Simone Weil pursued the deep and desperate love of God—all these and many, many more offer stories of faith, of spiritual direction and commitment to social transformation that can inform and attract the aspirations of New Age people.

The renewal of spiritual formation in Catholic and Protestant churches—as of yet too confined to seminaries, religious professionals, and elites—is a largely untapped resource in addressing the New Agers. The joining of spirituality and social compassion is long overdue in the U.S. church. We now have at hand an extraordinarily rich opportunity with a generation of North Americans searching for a direction that is holistic and transformative and yet can be informed by a realism that hears also the deep distrust of the possibility for change that blights the idealism of most on the cultural left.

We may be at the edge of a new awakening among the cultural left and of a fruitful conversation between the New Age movement and Christian faith. At present the metaphor of journey is the one that offers the most hope for a fresh engagement in the doing of theology.

Mainline churches, however, do not approach the cultural left in a vacuum. Their largest numbers of members come from the cultural right, the most heavily populated lifestyle grouping in the United States. These folk, too, will be a part of the future. These are the concerns of Part Three.

► Part Three ◄

*The
Cultural
Right*

▸5◂

Who Are the Cultural Right?

When I left high school in 1953 and went away to the university, I began a process of alienation from my roots that would proceed unabated for the next thirty years. Going to the university would be a life-altering experience. For one thing I found myself in an environment where a set of rules was in place that I not only did not know but did not have the social skills to employ if I had. Expectations of etiquette that were extraordinarily unstated in application were nevertheless power- fully enforced by measures as various as derisive laughter, arctic dismissal, and just plain dead air. The language was different too. One senior kept using the word "pseudo." He talked about pseudo- intellectuals, pseudoscience, pseudoreligionists, pseudopoliticians, and so forth, ad nauseam. I distinctly remember thinking that "pseudo" must be a powerfully useful word. My pronounced disappointment came later when I looked it up to discover that it only meant "phony."

The longer I pursued higher education, the more I noticed that I was picking up the rules and learning how to obfuscate my vocabulary so that my training "showed." Some of us learned to ape our professors and speak at the very front of our teeth, displaying, we hoped, the precision we found in our professors' lectures. Or we developed gestures of head or body that distinguished our communication with its obvi- ously educated flair. Yet these were only the more overt changes. Deeply stained into my consciousness was a new way of life, and I feared that my real roots would creep up out of the ground at any moment and send my pseudo tree of culture crashing into the verdant garden of the academic world. These changes of consciousness, however, were more permanent than I thought, and the alienation from my roots was gen- uine.

Please understand, there was a great deal I needed to be alienated from—my racism, my classism, my sexism, my love of violence, my militaristic patriotism, my narrow loyalties, and on and on. Yet I also felt, even then, that I was being alienated from some things that were of life-giving value and had an authentic human clarity, the loss of which represented some ineffable loss of soul.

My parents could see it but could not quite name it, although I remember my father once saying, "Well, son, you just keep on and you're gonna get so far out in front of us we're gonna mistake you for the enemy and shoot ya!"

Life-making, Territorially Rooted Locals

I had grown up on the cultural right of the United States, and no surer exit from it can be found than higher education and its fateful career compulsivities. The *first* day on campus my new roommate, Ed Butler, asked me what my career plans were. The question staggered me, since I didn't really think or talk much in those terms.

"Oh, I'm gonna play baseball for a living," I answered. I had escaped to L.S.U. seeking to avoid some inexplicable bump in the night that kept pushing me in the direction of the ministry.

"I mean really," he said, with such authority that I wondered if he had seen me play ball. Feeling flushed out of my illusions, I reversed the question to get out of the line of visibility. "Well, what are yours?"

"Oh, I intend to graduate here as a premed with a three point three or better, do my residence at Charity Hospital in New Orleans, and go back to practice medicine with my father in north Louisiana."

I can remember the devastating alchemy of being both impressed and intimidated. You see, people on the cultural right tend to be far less oriented to pursuing a career. That someone like Ed would have plans of such clarity was something I had heard about, of course, but it was something other people did, not I. Cultural-right people have to be— usually of necessity—far more focused on just making life come out right: providing enough for the family, making ends meet, doing what has to be done to the house or saving to buy one if possible. Life itself is enough to do. For this reason, among others, Richard Flacks has said that such folk are more interested in making life than in making history.

I once took a course at Harvard with Paul Tillich, the great German theologian who went to Union Theological Seminary in New York City in 1933. After his retirement from Union, he taught at Harvard for several years. The course consisted of his reading to us the manuscript that would become Part V of *Systematic Theology*, "History and the Kingdom of God."[1] One afternoon he particularly caught my attention when he said with passion, "History moves to an end, and zie end of history is zie kingdom of Gott; und Man is a history-making, history-bearing creature." Later in the summer I went home to Mississippi and, wanting to impress my father with my new theological learning, I announced, "Dad, did you know that man is a history-making, history-bearing creature?"

"Aw, [bleep], boy!" was his showstopping response.

Cultural-right people are territorially rooted. That small town or rural community or metropolitan neighborhood they live in is *the* center of meaning and value. It is the greatest place in the world to live: "There's no other place like it." My father and mother have asked me for thirty years when I was coming back *home* to stay. When I tell them Kansas City *is* my home and I'm not likely to leave it, they let me know that Brookhaven most certainly is my home, *not* Kansas City, and I should never forget it!

Oriented so powerfully to place, they are what Robert Merton called "locals," people whose frame of reference, whose central focus of concern, is the local community.[2] Martinez-Brawley defines localism as attachment to locality and as favoring what is local. In her discussion, which is about rural people, she is careful to explain that rural people neither maintain the total self-sufficiency of an isolated rural community nor reject certain national policies, such as Social Security or interstate highways. The preference for location does not necessarily mean a rejection of such national programs.[3]

It is important to understand that the people of the cultural right have considerable diversity within themselves. While locally oriented and territorially rooted, they are not one simplistic, homogeneous group. One major reason for these differences within the cultural right has to do with the sharp inequalities that occur even within this distinctively less privileged lifestyle grouping. While the cultural right is made up of the lower middle class, the working class, and the poor, the economic differences within this large group have considerable effect on their lifestyles. Racial and gender factors also have considerable impact, along with the factor of class.

For this reason some distinctions need to be made within the cultural right in order to be sufficiently alert to the character of what is the largest lifestyle grouping in the United States.

Respectables. The largest subgroup on the cultural right is what I call Respectables. The great bulk of the lower middle class, a significant number of blue-collar people, and those poor people who struggle hard to be loyal to standards of respectability make up this group. For such people respectability is the way they prove the success of their families and their lives. While ours is an achievement culture in terms of its basic commitments to success and winning, the chances of being a winner in our culture are small for most people. Hence, respectability is a compensative value, an alternative way of appraising one's dignity. Respectables are primarily carriers of the mixture of self-denial and respectability I attempted to characterize in some of the foregoing narratives. Respectables are profoundly family-oriented as well and cannot finally be understood unless one takes this orientation into account, as we shall see.

Arnold Mitchell, who names this group Belongers, reports that they tend to be older than average and are deeply devoted to traditional values, including not only the family but their local community, faith, and flag. Indeed, they are intensely patriotic and provide, without question, the shock troops for most churches. Mitchell's Belongers represent 60 million Americans, the largest single lifestyle group, one of every three U.S. adults. They are sentimental and tough with an abiding stability and strength. Having a median income below the national figure (in 1986 the median family income for whites was $30,809 and, for blacks, $19,832), most of those in this lifestyle are female (68 percent). Half of them have less than a high school education.[4]

On the cultural right one can also find a small minority of wealthy people. Some of them use their wealth to promote a joining of laissez faire capitalism and traditional values. This, however, is an uneasy alliance, as we shall see.

Hard Living. A second subgroup on the cultural right is made up of those who are into "hard living," as Joseph T. Howell once described their behavior. In his study of a group of such hard-living people outside Washington, D.C., he concluded that they were people who did a lot of heavy drinking, experienced a lot of marital instability, and were tough, politically alienated, rootless, oriented in the present, and deeply committed to an individualism that prizes independence and self-reliance.[5]

In more recent research Arnold Mitchell calls this lifestyle "Sustainers." He discovered that they are "angry, distrustful, rebellious, anxious people who often feel left out of things."[6] Beyond survival but still near-poor, hard-living people struggle to keep the little they have. With a median income of nearly half the national figure, they are often unemployed, with more than a fourth of their number seeking employment or working part-time. Their jobs are not satisfying and are typically semiskilled or unskilled: work with machines, manual labor, and a range of service occupations. Understandably, they are the least satisfied with their financial condition of any of Mitchell's lifestyle groups, and they are most anxious to improve their material circumstances. The Hard Living have both large families and a high proportion (20 percent) of people who are divorced, separated, or living together unmarried. A high percentage of minorities (13 percent Hispanic and 21 percent black) are represented among the Hard Living. Acutely aware of their low social status, they rank next to the bottom in personal happiness and deeply mistrust the system, having little confidence in politicians and corporate managers.

Mitchell also found several clear types of subgroups in this life-style: (1) the "street-smart operator" found in the central cities of the United States, who knows how to work the underground criminal economy; (2) "the crafty Sustainer," not so much involved in criminal pursuits, who knows how to work the system through trade-offs, cash jobs done on the side, and sometimes a stealthy maneuvering of welfare programs; (3) the poverty-stricken Sustainer family, usually a single mother with children scratching out a meager living by parlaying a minimum wage job, food stamps, and, when possible, welfare; and (4) the immigrant, new to the United States, with a minimal command of English, few relevant skills, and sometimes without family or friends, but highly motivated, disciplined, industrious, and believing that the system is responsive to his or her striving.

Hard Living people want more from life and expect more; they plan for it and seek it out; yet they do not trust people, are not happy, and feel excluded from things. Some will eventually make it to other lifestyle subgroups where life will be better, even if not affluent and prestigious.[7]

The Desperate Poor. The third subgroup on the cultural right consists of those 6 million Americans who constitute the poorest of the poor. Their income never exceeds 40 percent of the national median income, and nearly 80 percent receive less than a fourth of that. They are old, with an average age of sixty-six, often ill and poorly educated. Little wonder that they are "despairing, withdrawn, mistrustful, rebellious about their situation, lacking in self-confidence, and finding little satisfaction in any aspect of their lives." They struggle to survive, to avoid utter loss and the shrinking whirlpool of blocked opportunity and old age. Overwhelmed by the world they know, they seek shelter in the fantasies of television. They are "traditional, conservative, conventional and believe more than all other groups that the world is changing too fast."[8]

Mitchell finds two distinct classes among the Desperate Poor ("Survivors," he calls them). The one is made up of those who are trapped in intergenerational poverty. Rarely do they escape it. More than that, the pervasive testimony of their experience is that escape is closed off to them, certainly by any of the usual means. In this class of Survivors is a high proportion of ethnics who live mostly in city ghettos or isolated rural communities. The ethnics in this class tend to be younger than the aged poor. The other class of Survivors has slipped into this condition by virtue of misfortune, a lack of effort, or the impoverishing effects of old age from which they could not protect themselves. In their younger years they were Respectables and Hard Living. These people tend to be white and older and to have more resources, especially in the form of a home. Some continue to live in the aging frame houses of the rural and urban United States; others have gone to nursing homes. Survivors are 77 percent female, testifying again to the feminization of poverty.[9]

There is a basic difference between the Hard Living and the Desperate Poor, on the one hand, and Respectables, on the other. The former, poor and near-poor, are need-driven, while the latter, more comfortable, are outer-directed and respectability seeking. Respectables are far more apt to be in church, and the Hard Living and Desperate Poor much less so. Yet I include all three lifestyles on the cultural right, because of their highly local orientations. I must confess, however, some ambivalence about placing the Hard Living here because of their ambition and desire for status, which give them a kinship with the cultural middle. They have the dreams, but they do not have the opportunity and the necessary wherewithal.[10]

In short, the cultural right is made up of most farmers, blue-collar workers, the lower middle class, the poor, and the near-poor. The Respectables believe deeply in the self-denial ethic described earlier, and they believe in respectability. The crush of their impoverished reality has made respectability irrelevant for most of the Desperate Poor, and the hustling behavior and ambition of the Hard Living place such a compensative value on a back burner as they strive to reach their dreams. Because in mainline churches the overwhelming presence of the cultural right will be that of Respectables, probably 40 to 50 percent of most churches, attention in what follows will be more directly focused on them. In fact, in many churches in urban and rural areas the task is to get Respectables to be concerned about and to provide services and take action on behalf of the Hard Living and the Desperate Poor.

Respectables are astounded by the lifestyles of the cultural left. They are either confused and dismayed by it or consumed by anger against it. When Jerry Falwell attacked the "secular humanism" of the culture, he was reaching for a large group of Americans who want little to do with the inner-directed self-fulfillment lifestyles of many of today's young adults.[11] Yet, basically, the Respectables are a contented lot, satisfied and supportive of their way of life.

Religion and the Cultural Right

Powerful tendencies operate in U.S. society to stereotype people on the cultural right, especially those who are religious. They tend to be seen as a group of rock-ribbed fundamentalists who hold to a set of mindless propositions about Christian faith and want to reverse the findings of contemporary science and destroy civil liberties and rights except those that defend *their* religious practices. Such a stereotype certainly does not fit the great majority of people on the cultural right and is not accurate or fair, for that matter, to most fundamentalists. It may therefore be helpful to sort out something of the religious landscape of the cultural right in order to arrive at a more accurate understanding of who they are.

Perhaps the largest single group, religiously, would be the evangelicals. With evangelicals defined as those who would affirm that they (1) are born again, (2) believe in the literal truth of scripture, and (3) have witnessed and attempted to bring others to Christ, evangelicals represent about one fifth of the adult American population. Using this survey finding, one could say that evangelicals constitute some 35 million people in the United States.[12]

Evangelicals themselves are not a monolith. Fowler found a continuum of evangelicals that involved radical reform evangelicals, mainstream evangelicals and fundamentalists.[13] Hunter reports that a sizable group of evangelicals are the new young evangelicals who have their social roots in the new class.[14] Obviously, with these diversities within evangelical ranks, some fall outside the cultural right. Nevertheless, perhaps as many as half of all evangelicals would be cultural right.

Fundamentalists also compose a significant number of people on the cultural right. Ammerman distinguishes fundamentalists from evangelicals by three basic characteristics: (1) their separation from the world, (2) dispensational premillennialism, and (3) biblical literalism. She also notes that fundamentalism has not accepted the cognitive style of modernity in the way that evangelicals have, which includes functional rationality, structural pluralism, and cultural pluralism. Significantly, she observes that fundamentalism exists at those places where tradition and modernity are in conflict rather than at those where modernity is absent. She makes an important distinction between fundamentalists in urban centers and those who live in essentially traditional communities, noting that the latter may share many beliefs and practices with their conservative urban cousins but do not share the militant separatism that characterizes fundamentalism as a movement. Persons in traditional communities may score high on orthodoxy, literalism, or "evangelicalism," but she argues that in "significant ways traditional, rural, often Southern, religion is different in kind from the religious expressions of people who must encounter diversity every day. Only where traditional orthodoxy must defend itself against modernity does fundamentalism truly emerge."[15] Roof estimates that hard-core fundamentalists constitute about one third of the evangelicals in the United States.[16]

Evangelicals and fundamentalists do not, however, constitute the whole of the cultural right. Hill makes four distinctions in Southern religion that would characterize the cultural right more broadly in the United States. He describes fundamentalists as "truth-oriented," evangelicals as "conversion-oriented," devotionalists as "spiritually oriented," and ethical types as "service-oriented." These four types expand the range of religious orientations in the cultural right.[17] I would add to that a number of people who fit none of these categories but who are the conservative, respectable, churchgoing, denominationally identified Americans who constitute a sizable number of the cultural right.

All these types of persons are distributed among various denominations in the United States. Membership in some denominations, such as independent Baptist churches, includes large numbers of fundamentalists. Evangelicals, however, can be found distributed—although unevenly—across all denominations. The point is that the cultural right is religiously quite diverse and this diversity of groups is spread widely across the various mainline and conservative churches, except in those places where denominations are made up almost exclusively of fundamentalists and evangelicals. Mainline denominations have significant numbers of cultural right persons and substantial representation from respectable, conservative churchgoers. Roman Catholics would also have a large representation from the cultural right. With their long history of an immigrant membership and large proportions of white ethnic and working-class people their churches would continue to have a significant presence of locally oriented, socio-morally conservative Respectables and certainly not a few of the Hard Living and the Desperate Poor who identify themselves as Catholic.

Politics and the Cultural Right

The stereotypes of the cultural right are nowhere as dense as they are around political issues. Though they are viewed by many as rock-ribbed, neolithic authoritarians, with a lowbrow mentality that provides fertile ground for Hitlerian reactionary forces, it is surprising to most to learn that this simply has never been true.

First of all, the cultural right is not the stronghold of reactionary political forces in the United States. The lower middle class, for example, was found by Hamilton to be more often Democratic than the college-educated upper middle class and more liberal on medical care and standard of living issues than these same affluent and successful Americans.[18] The fact is that the stronghold of U.S. conservatism is among upper-middle-class business and professional people, not the lower middle class. The portrayal of the latter as "distinctly reactionary and compulsively moralistic" does not hold up under careful scrutiny.[19] With respect to blue collarites the research is more mixed, but this reflects not only a bias in the research but a failure to understand at close quarters what is really going on.

Second, the cultural right is typically depicted as authoritarian. In 1950 Adorno and associates defined an authoritarian personality as rigid, intolerant, suspicious, and punitive, who saw the world in either-or, all-or-nothing terms and loathed "deviants." Strength and toughness were vaunted. Interestingly enough, in Adorno's work the concept of the authoritarian personality was used to account for the middle-class basis of fascism.[20] It was Seymour M. Lipset who extended the concept to cover working-class people. They were seen as intolerant and opposed to civil rights and liberties. These authoritarian traits grew out of deficiencies in blue-collar life in education, organizational participation, finances, and authoritarian families.[21] Stereotyping grew from such theory and found wide currency among social scientists, intellectuals, and pop savants.

Subsequent study, however, found more deficiencies in that early research than in the people under investigation.[22] In 1974 Lillian Rubin reported that working-class people she interviewed were not like the "inarticulate, simple-minded, asocial, sexually repressed, family-centered, authoritarian stereotype."[23] In fact, their views on international issues and questions of war and peace were much more complex. While working people generally opposed friendly relations with the Communists, they were more ready than others to pull out of Vietnam and move toward a compromise to end the war. The hard-nosed, belligerent attitude toward the war came from educated upper-class and middle-class Protestants. Moreover, authoritarian attitudes on civil rights were not the result of a working-class background per se but of religious and regional factors where intolerance was associated with Southerners and Protestants.[24] Another study found no significant difference among seven occupational groups except for the greater tolerance among clerical workers. Educational level was much more related to tolerance.[25]

What seems to have been missing from research on blue collarites is a more sympathetic approach to how they see the world.[26] Their punitive attitudes toward student demonstrators and black civil rights activists, for example, grew more from their respect for authority, commitment to the American dream, resentment over society's neglect of their own needs, and feelings of powerlessness. The concrete conditions and strains of their own lives rather than the dynamics of prejudiced, authoritarian personalities gave rise to their views. Other research details a range of such grievances that are in keeping with this interpretation.[27]

Let me be very clear about my report of this research and my reasons for it. It is not my contention that working people are free of racism. This is a racist society, and white working people are responsible for that along with other whites. My concern is that stereotypes about working-class whites tend to promote the view that racism is located primarily with them and with other authoritarian personalities. Such stereotyping relieves upper-status types who may know how to avoid a prejudicial answer in a questionnaire or to maintain discreet languaging about ethnics in polite conversation, but at the same time they (we!) resist through complex, sanctioned, institutionalized racism the movement of ethnics into suburbia; block higher-management jobs to ethnics and Jews in the primary corporate sector of the economy; pass a host of mortgage and tax laws for personal benefit; and draw more material welfare from the government than do the poor or the working class.[28]

Moreover, racism, sexism, and classism are internally related. Stereotyping, whether on the basis of ethnicity, gender, or class, nourishes oppression in the United States. Transformative change is not assisted by classist scapegoating.

To return to the political views of the cultural right, the survey of research just reported is further corroborated by Arnold Mitchell's work. Among Belongers (Respectables) nearly half (49 percent) are Democrats; 23 percent are Republicans and 28 percent Independent. Forty-four percent are middle-of-the-road, 46 percent are conservative, and 10 percent are liberal. While this is certainly no liberal group, it is a more moderate group than the professional and managerial cultural middle, where two thirds of the Achievers are conservative, with political views we will discuss later.

Survivors (the Desperate Poor) are the most conservative lifestyle group on the cultural right, where 53 percent are conservative, 28 percent middle-of-the-road, and 19 percent liberal. Sixty percent are Democratic and only 15 percent Republican. The remaining 25 percent are Independent.

The Sustainers (the Hard Living) are the most moderate to liberal group on the cultural right: middle-of-the-road, 48 percent; liberal, 23 percent; and conservative, 29 percent. They are much more Democratic (50 percent) and Independent (41 percent) than Republican (9 percent).[29]

In terms of their moderate to conservative bent, one other distinction is quite important: that of socio-moral conservatism vis-à-vis politico-economic conservatism. Research for some time has revealed that cultural-right people tend to be conservative on such socio-moral issues as abortion, school prayer, the women's movement, gay/lesbian rights, and the ERA. Yet, as we have seen, they tend to be more mixed with a majority that is moderate to liberal on political and economic issues. Why is this so? It is because the conservatism of cultural-right people comes from their commitment to traditional values in the family and kinship ties. Their conservatism is not rooted in a primary commitment to laissez-faire capitalism.

Rebecca Klatch demonstrates this quite clearly in her research on new right women. She discovered a very sharp difference between socio-morally conservative women and those committed to laissez-faire economics. The former see the world from a religious perspective, more specifically from a Christian or Judeo-Christian view of morality. At the center of their world is the family, the basic institution of society on which everything else is built, as they see it. Essential in this ordering of the world is the authority of the family, which inculcates children with solid morals and keeps rein on the self-interested pursuits growing from human egoism, especially as this characterizes men when unrestrained by family commitments, religious faith, and traditional values. In their view America is in moral decay, and the family is under threat of devastation. The task before the socio-morally conservative woman, then, is the restoration of America, a rebirth of religious faith, morality, and decency, and America's return to being the righteous land of the founding fathers.

Laissez-faire conservative women see the world not from the perspective of religion but from that of liberty, explicitly "the economic liberty of the free market and the political liberty based on the minimal state."[30]

Based on the classic liberalism of Smith, Locke, and Mill, liberty and individualism are inextricably joined so that the basic entity of society is not the family but "the autonomous, rational, self-interested individual." Possessing free will, initiative, and self-reliance, the individual has the task of pursuing his or her self-interest confident that the "invisible hand" will provide a natural harmony. Here the greatest good resides not in a traditional social order rooted in a moral authority that restrains self-interest. Rather, a truly free society authorizes the individual to pursue opportunity in the context of a competitive order with the aim of nourishing creativity and productivity. The place of America in history, then, is to be the "cradle of liberty." These conservatives, too, believe that the United States is in trouble, not because of moral corruption but because of the "erosion of liberty." In America's turn from the limited state and the free market the economic and political liberty of the individual is under dire threat. Hence, for laissez-faire conservatives economic issues and national defense are the top issues on the nation's agenda.

It is crucial to understand that the overwhelming majority of people on the cultural right do not participate in the New Political Right. Yet, even in a study of New Right activists this sharp dichotomy between socio-moral and politico-economic conservatives still holds. More than that, Klatch's work is a study of activists who tend to be more affluent and better educated: that is, people more likely to be in the cultural middle. Yet her research found that, even among activists, social conservatives are closer, in age, education, religion, marital status, and occupation, to what I call cultural right.[31]

If one is to understand the cultural right, it is necessary to see this distinction between socio-moral and politico-economic conservatism.

The reasons for socio-moral conservatism are rooted in the local net-works. I believe that the nature and the sources of their commitments make people on the cultural right open to change and that indeed they can be an important group in leading the United States toward change. We turn to this in the next chapter.

►6◄

Doing Ministry on the Cultural Right

I have been struck for many years now by how differently people on the cultural right approach religious faith and social issues from those of the cultural left and the cultural middle. The more I have attempted to learn from people of the cultural right, the more convinced I am that those of us trained in the universities and the seminaries are socialized into a way of relating to the world that makes us unfit for working on the cultural right. It is not only the vocabulary or the personal tastes. It is not only our cosmopolitanism, on the one hand, or their localism, on the other, at least not on the surface. It certainly is not because those on the cultural right are ignorant or cannot think or lack the sensitivity found in most college graduates. My suspicion is that basic cognitive ability, emotional depth, moral and spiritual maturity, and wisdom are fairly evenly distributed across cultural lifestyles and social classes. The notion that the cream rises to the top is true only of unhomogenized milk; it is blatantly misleading as a way to account for the distribution of wealth, achievement, status, and power. This cartoon depiction of American life would be laughable were it not so ideologically useful to the privileged and so internally and individualistically believed by those who make up the overwhelming majority of the American people.

Moreover, in the church we have made an awesome mistake by trying to legitimate efforts in the direction of liberation, justice, and peace by using a rationale that may be compelling to the university-trained—at least some of them—but leaves a chasm between professional church leaders and cultural-right people.

Yet it is worse than that. Most university-trained people and most seminary professors do not find culturally right people interesting. It is rare, in my experience, for academics to see the cultural right as an arena of intellectually stimulating research and study. Most students are no different. Over two decades of seminary teaching I typically find white students, for example, who are very much interested in the traditional subcultures of blacks, Hispanics, and Native Americans—for which I rejoice—yet have no interest at all in the traditional subcultures of white people, who constitute the majority of the cultural right in the United States.

In fact, most who come *from* the cultural right seem hell-bent to escape it; they find studying it an unsettling remembrance of a world they hope will fade into the distance as they board the jet plane of higher education for worlds more worthy of their ambition. One of the problems of such disengagement is that they also give away a basic part of who they are. To refuse to claim one's origins is plainly and simply a loss of self.

Many seminarians adopt interests and tastes through education that block their interest in and capacity to relate to the majority of the people in their churches, especially in the early part of their careers. One man in his mid-twenties said to me, "Sample, you didn't tell me what it was like. You didn't tell me how alien I would feel."

I protested, reminding him that I had worked through such things with the class, that over and over we had discussed and attempted to understand the cultural right. All my protestations, however, were to no avail.

"You didn't tell me, Sample, you couldn't!"

We find ourselves in a time when higher education unfits us for work with the cultural right and leads us to perceive professional assignment among them as a mission in alien and—unfortunately—dull country.

Yet it does not have to be so. The study of the cultural right is a pursuit of labyrinthine complexity that offers an opportunity for mission and professional ministry as lively and challenging as any other. It does require, however, some retraining and a willingness to relearn old ways of thinking and the means to address important questions in an approach consistent with the circumstances of their lives. My job here is to outline some of the key dimensions of this approach and how it can work on the cultural right. If we can learn a more effective way to relate, we have an opportunity to work with the cultural right in ways that communicate respect and understanding. While this is no easy task, it is an invigorating one, leading to a new world for some and opening up a long-closed door for those who grew up there but walked away.

Traditional Values

Basic to the approach to meaning of cultural-right people are traditional values: family, home, neighborhood or community, faith, and flag. These values are often the object of demeaning jokes and, in some instances, withering hostility. When I told one man that I intended to write a manuscript in praise of the virtues of traditional values, he actually became enraged and in imperial tones instructed me to find another topic!

I believe that those holding such views have not examined carefully enough the concrete, lived reality of people on the cultural right and the ways in which these values promote and defend the very relationships that make life possible and give it meaning.

Family

The family is, of course, a central institution in American life. Not many people find it unimportant. For those in successful business and professional lives, though, the priority of the family is often rivaled by career. Many are pressed to make hard choices between what is best for the family and what is best for career advancement. But the great majority on the cultural right do not have careers, as such; they have skills or jobs if they are blue-collar; they have a farm, not a career, if they are farmers; and their low-scale positions in the lower middle class do not usually take on the paramount significance they tend to have for the cultural middle. Hence, the family is the major preoccupation of the cultural right. Important questions and issues are those that impact the family, and the evaluation of a social question, if it is to receive more than passing conversational interest, will be evaluated in terms of its effects on the family. Thus, to talk about a social issue in terms of the universals of a cosmopolitan framework is simply to miss cultural-right people where they live. To mount up evidence in terms of the findings of economics or social science or legal precedent or theological tradition or ethical analysis that does not deal directly with family life as experienced in a locally lived kinship setting does not connect at a crucial point in the understanding of cultural-right people.

Back in the days when Anita Bryant was leading the forces in Florida against an ordinance granting certain rights to gay and lesbian persons, I went home to visit my mother and father in Mississippi. In their house the TV goes on first thing in the morning and goes off at bedtime. Throughout the day one eats in front of it, has conversation in front of it, and entertains company in front of it. It is the ever-present companion, even if it is not always the central focus of attention.

My first morning there the TV was on, and Mama and I were having a genuinely delightful conversation which I was enjoying very much. Suddenly, on the tube appears Ms. Bryant making a speech against gay and lesbian rights. Now, you need to understand that I'm one of that minority of Americans who believes that homosexuality is created by God, is not a sin or a pathology, and needs and deserves greater institutional support in our society. You will not be surprised, I suspect, to know that my mother does not usually agree with me about such things.

When Ms. Bryant appeared on the TV, I just froze. Every muscle tightened, because I knew there would be an argument. My mother said in a loud voice, "That hussy ought to shut her mouth!"

My head snapped around, and I sat there with my mouth gaping in utter incredulity. Mama noticed my expression and turned her high-volume outrage toward me.

"Well, what are you looking at? I suppose *you* like her!"

"Well, Mama, I don't know whether I like her or not, I don't *know* her, but I certainly disagree with her. I'm just surprised that you don't like her point of view either." I said, halting between phrases and picking my words with the caution of one dismantling a time bomb.

"Well, I don't like her, and I don't like what she's sayin' and doin'."

"Why?" I asked gently.

"They've hurt those people enough. They've just hurt 'em and hurt 'em, and it ain't right. It just ain't right. Now, you take that poor boy, Roger, he ain't never done nothin' to nobody, but they ain't done nothin' but hurt that boy and hurt that boy. It ain't right and they ought to stop it, and that hussy ought to shut her mouth."

At the time of this occurrence, Roger was no boy. He was a fifty-three-year-old man, but that didn't matter to my mother, who was much older. And, if you have a popular stereotype of a gay man, Roger probably fits it. Very effeminate, he dressed swish in those days and was a hairdresser, but these things did not matter to my mother either. What did matter was the fact that Roger was the brother of my mother's best friend. If you mess with my mother's family or her friend's family, you have cut down more hay than you can pick up in three seasons.

I could have engaged my mother at that time in a conversation about homosexuality, and I could have marshaled my arguments in good cosmopolitan fashion. I could have said, Mother, are you aware that the American Psychiatric Association has taken homosexuality off its list of mental disorders? And she would have replied, shouting, Well, they're a bunch of Communists anyhow!

I would simply have blown the whole thing. The way to discuss that issue, or any issue like it, is to work it through the kinship or friendship relations a person or a group has. Such an approach talks the language of the cultural right and honors the key relationships of their lives. Please understand, I do not see this as a panacea. Cultural-right people may still disagree with one's point of view even when it is argued from their approach to meaning. The point, rather, is that to have any real chance of being persuasive, of getting a hearing, one will do well to work the relationship of family and the effect of issues on it.

Neighborhood or Community

"Neighborhood" is a loaded word in our society. It has been used in obscenely racist ways and has been the legitimative slogan of some of the worst demagogues in the country. It has also been used in humanely just ways. A community organization in Boston once organized blacks and whites together in behalf of better neighborhoods even in the aftermath of a bitter busing conflict.[1]

For a people who are local in orientation, the neighborhood or community is the locus of the deepest relationships of their lives. Often they have extended family there and friendships that go back decades. They may very well have attended the schools their children or grand-children now attend. Their churches may be buildings where they were baptized and married, or where they buried their parents, a spouse, or a child. The store owners and merchants may be old friends. Local cafés and bars are centers for gathering where they are bonded and rebonded to people and place. Hence, the importance of that local place is not because of some ignorant parochialism or stubborn refusal to look beyond it. These local settings and their relationships populate the very story of their lives. To ignore the reality of this is to ignore and discount them. To dismiss the place is to demean the people.

In the approach to meaning of the cultural right, then, the neighborhood or community is a pivotal dimension for assessing issues and evaluating the response to them. Recently, I was in a local church in Iowa listening to a pastor talk to a group of urbanites about the issue of housing. In an aside, he mentioned the attempts by Yonkers, New York, residents to keep low-income housing out of their community. He indicated that in his opinion the community would be stronger if it had low-income people there. He was immediately pressed by two men in the room.

"Wait a minute," one said. "If I spend hard-earned money on a house in a nice neighborhood, why do I have to accept people like that who lower my property values, and why do I have to accept people I just don't want to live next to?"

The pastor on first instinct made a terrible error that almost lost him the opportunity to be persuasive with them. He suggested that we need diversity and pluralism in our communities. They both went after him. "Why can't we have a neighborhood that welcomes a certain group of people if we want it?"

The pastor, quick on his feet, saved himself.

"Look, here's what I mean: I grew up in a small farming town. There was one millionaire farmer in that whole county, but you would never have known it. He wore khaki work clothes and drove a pickup truck. He looked and acted like everyone else. The farmer next to him was poor, but they neighbored together and were friends. America at its best used to be like that. We were Americans and we were neighbors, and we didn't try to separate ourselves from each other by how much money we made. If we lose those kinds of neighborhoods and communities, something very precious will be lost, and America won't be the same."

I was amazed. Both men stopped their argument as though reminded of something they had forgotten. They were not frustrated and angry; they just seemed to understand. The pastor's praise of pluralism and diversity—empty abstractions to people on the cultural right—took on a very different meaning when reworked through the history of their own communities. Both of those men remembered. To reject the pastor's observation at that point was to throw out the flesh and blood and place of their own histories.

Love of Country

I was taught in seminary to be very suspicious of the nation-state. People have a great propensity to idolize it, to make it god and fall down in worship before it. It is wise to practice a hermeneutics of suspicion when dealing with the nation-state. At the same time, as Alan Geyer once said to me, unless one has an appropriate love of country one cannot have an adequate theology of culture.[2] Some of our nation's most charismatic leaders seemed to understand this. Walter Wink observes that Martin Luther King, Jr., never attacked the soul of America but rather called it to live out its deepest dreams.[3]

Such things are important to realize when working with the cultural right. John Schaar has said that love of country for such folk is a profound sense of gratitude for the country, its people, symbols, history, and meaning.[4] Therefore, when a cosmopolitan criticizes the country, he or she sounds like an ingrate, like someone who does not have a very basic quality that defines one as human. This love of country by the cultural right and their gratitude do not mean that they cannot be critical of the country. Their love of country is not necessarily idolatrous. For the most part cultural-right people know the difference between gratitude and idolatry. What they want to know is whether their pastor does.

Shortly after I had begun to name some of these approaches to meaning of cultural-right people, I was invited to preach a sermon on the issue of peace at a local church. The pastor indicated that he wanted me to say what was really in my heart. He wanted me to "lay it out." The church was a four-hour drive away, and I arrived at the parsonage about nine o'clock on Saturday night. He then told me, "By the way, Tex, this is really a 'hawk' church. Half the congregation is military, and the other half is a combination of skilled blue collarites and low-middle-class sales and service people. I thought you might want to know that before tomorrow." He chuckled as he contemplated my dilemma.

Fortunately, I had had an experience during the past year that floated up out of my memory as I sat in my motel wondering what in the world I would say to establish some kind of relationship with the congregation so I could be honest and forthright about the issue of peace.

The event I remembered began in Boston one bright sunshiny day when I heard on the radio that the United States was basically without cloud cover all the way across the continent. When I got to the airport, I managed to get a window seat with its view unimpeded by the wing. I then made a decision that I would keep my head in the window the entire flight to Los Angeles and that I would not turn away—except to look away occasionally to keep my neck from having muscle spasms— so long at any time that I could not look back and see the place I had last seen.

The plane took off from Logan Airport and banked out over the Atlantic. As we climbed, I could see the lobster claw that was Cape Cod. We turned across Massachusetts, flying west and a bit south. Crossing the beautiful Berkshires, I could see New York State with those magnificent forests and lakes. To the north the Great Lakes came into view and later, in the distance, Detroit and Chicago. Illinois flew under us, and the tip of Iowa lay just beyond the Mississippi. Then we flew across part of Nebraska, and eastern Colorado displayed that stretch of the Great Plains which even from that height seemed endless. Soon those extravagant Rockies came into view and seemed to clap their hands below. We flew within sight of Rocky Mountain National Park, and I lifted myself to peer across and see Pike's Peak standing to the south, seemingly quite aloof to the subjective praise I offered. As we left Colorado, I could see the so-called wasteland of Nevada, those seemingly endless rivuleted hills and ridges alone and infinite. Las Vegas looked sleepy as it spread below, recognizably there but not lit in the daylight hours, and, besides, it pleaded no contest before that huge sky and the changing, unexcelled beauty that flew past below. Suddenly there they were, the mountains of California, and the plane headed through a riflesight of San Bernardino peaks and across the valley below. Smoggy but visible that day, Los Angeles was racing toward us and dragging a sea of Pacific diamonds behind it. In a matter of four or five hours—I can't remember how long, it seems an instant—I saw America from sea to shining sea. One simply cannot do that and not love this land. From Boston to LA across field and forest, lakes and mountains, deserts and plains. The alabaster—from the distance—cities station themselves across the continent to give reason for the roads and highways running in every direction.

The next morning the sermon began with that story, and I used it to claim the beauty of other lands also, and the necessity of peace, the end of nuclear weapons, and the dream of a world without war. I said everything I wanted to say. Surely many people there disagreed with some, maybe most, of what I said, but they listened, and when the service ended I received what seemed to be genuine warmth from them and expressions of gratitude that did not seem contrived or forced. I do not think now—and did not think then—that this was some ringing evidence of my skill as a preacher or my oratorical power, and I promise not to tell even one other "success story" in this entire book, because what I saw happen was that I made contact with *their* approach to meaning, with *their* love of country, and in that context they trusted me enough to let me say things they otherwise would not have tolerated gladly.

Experiences and insights such as these have led me to reevaluate traditional values, their place in the lived reality of cultural-right people, and their possibilities for legitimating change in the direction of liberation and of justice. Unfortunately, people on both the political left and the political right have a common view of traditional values, believing, as they do, that such values support the status quo. For this reason the political right supports traditional values and the political left opposes them.

Richard Flacks, however, has demonstrated their potential for change and maintains that most of the great social movements of history were triggered by people who believed in traditional values, suspected that someone was out to subvert them, began to act to restore those values, and, in the process, brought about great change.[5]

Pastors and other social and religious leaders who are prepared to learn the ways that a logic of meaning makes use of traditional values can find an exciting ministry among people on the cultural right and will discover new horizons for social change and social justice opening before them.

I dare say that any woman with a consciousness of sexism would have sharply raised suspicions about my support of traditional values as sources of social change, especially with regard to the status and role of women. My point, however, is that a great deal can be done in terms of women's liberation through traditional values, but in the service of change rather than patriarchy.

Several years ago I was in conversation with two women, one a thirty-year-old who was very much a feminist and the other a fifty-six-year-old who was clearly cultural right. As we were standing there, the thirty-year-old said, "Did you see the paper today? Women still make sixty percent of what men do."

"Well, that's about right," said the older woman. "In fact, the sooner women get back home and stay there and let the men earn the living, the better off we will all be. Women need to stay home where they belong."

I just took one step back because I figured the younger woman would put on pole-climbing spikes and start up one leg of the older woman and come down the other side. I could not have been more wrong. Knowing that the older woman had been widowed early in her marriage and had a daughter she loved very much, the younger woman asked gently, "Is that what you want for your daughter?"

"It doesn't matter what I want. She'll just have to live with it. I did; she'll have to."

"I know, but is that what you *want* for your daughter?"

"Look, I had to work all my life. I *had* to do it that way. If I did it, she can."

"I know you did. You did it heroically. In fact, I don't know anyone who worked harder than you to make life good for your children, and your daughter will be able to face things because she's *your* daughter, if for no other reason. My question, though, is whether you want your daughter to have to struggle that way, to get only sixty percent of what a man does when she works at the same kind of job?"

The older woman melted. "No, I don't want it for my daughter. It's wrong, and it ought to be changed."

"That's what's really important," said the thirty-year-old. "We need to think about things like this in terms of people we love and see how they get hurt by them. These issues really boil down to personal and family issues."

I was stunned by the turnaround of the older woman and the way the younger woman kept up a sensitive, gentle focus on the issue from the standpoint of family values. She had the capacity to redefine the issue in terms of the concrete, lived relationships of the other woman and to push the issue in a way that made sense and drew her support.

It is crucial to understand that these kinds of family relationships are among the most powerful for people on the cultural right. To propose new directions for understanding or action will require a faithfulness to these relationships and the demonstration that a new way of doing things makes life better and promotes the health of these relationships. What must be avoided is an interpretation of traditional values that is oppressive and contrary to the needs and rightful interests of those on the cultural right and others. If one means by traditional values that victims of inequality, oppression, and exploitation are to remain in subservient positions, then obviously traditional values must be opposed. My contention, however, is that traditional values grow out of valuable relationships on the cultural right for which there is a genuine concern to make and keep these relationships healthy, just, and whole.

To move in a transformative direction when working with the cultural right involves an imaging and direction of the social change that depicts its positive impact on these deep ties and their vital nourishment. It is, clearly, the most effective way to legitimate change and to find the sustained motivation to carry it through. As we continue to look at the cultural right, further development and illustration of these matters will be forthcoming.

These traditional values, however, are only one aspect of the logic of meaning. We now turn to another, that of conventional morality.

Conventional Morality

When I was the pastor of a small blue-collar congregation, I was concerned to find some kind of study program that would attract the youth and be genuinely useful to them. I came up with the idea of doing a course on sexuality. Well, the young people came in large numbers, and the course was an instant success. At about that time I was trying to get my mind around contextual ethics, with the idea that principles and norms were helpful in ethics but that rules per se were not fully adequate in dealing with morality, including sexual morality. Part of the reason, I noted, was that the rules were sometimes in conflict. I said these kinds of things to the young people, trying to be careful not to sound like a libertine but simply to acknowledge the complexity of moral choices. These young people, of course, would go home and share my views with their parents. Within several days one of the mothers came to see me.

"Mr. Sample, I need to say something to you. I want you to know I do like you and appreciate what you are trying to do to help the young people, but you are saying some things about morals that are very dangerous. You see, you have a college education, and you finished the seminary. In a couple of years you will have one of them piled higher and deeper [a Ph.D.], and by then you will go on to a bigger and better job. But most of our young people will graduate from high school and get themselves a job making about half what you do. And when a person talks about morality the way you do, that can get young people like ours in a lot of trouble. You see, Mr. Sample, you have to have money to believe in morals the way you do. Most of our young people will never be able to afford the kind of life you talk about. It gets too expensive when you get in trouble."

At one level, it does not matter whether she fully understood my basic position or not. What is important is to understand *hers*. My attempt to talk with the young people about the relational character of values sounded to her like relativ*ism*, and she knew how hard it was to make ends meet, to keep family and home together, and to avoid "trouble." She also had some idea of what it would cost to hire an attorney if a young person got entangled with the law, or how difficult it was for a teenage couple to make a living after an early shotgun wedding, or how financially disastrous a divorce would be. In this social context the clarity of the rules, the need for sexual restraint, and the wisdom of conventional morality were clear. In her world and that of most of those young people my ethical views might have been academically correct, but they were circumstantially out of touch with working-class realities. That the sexual revolution was already under way and that the new morality of the 60's counterculture would soon radically affect blue-collar young people like these do not affect the sagacity of her position. One only has to look at the impact of such views on those who cannot "afford" them to understand the substantive strength of what she said.

The point is that conventional morality must be understood in terms of the social circumstances in which it arises. Those on the cultural right are people who live out their lives within the confines of stringent to moderate financial constraint.

More than this, however, is the fact that when something does go wrong, people of the cultural right are thrown back on the kinship ties and local friendships that form the durable support on which they depend. The research of Jerome L. Himmelstein is instructive here. His study of women who opposed the Equal Rights Amendment found that they wanted equality with men in terms of equal pay for equal work, equal treatment before the law, and the like, but that they opposed the ERA itself because they are basically opposed to too much individual autonomy. Why?

Himmelstein found that these antifeminist locally oriented women tend to come out of religious networks, whereas the proponents of ERA do not. In fact, religious participants, whatever the denomination, are more likely to be opponents of ERA and abortion for two reasons. First, their religious participation places them in a culture that holds to traditional images of women and the family. Second, these churches connect them to networks that can be readily mobilized by social movements. In contrast, the women *for* ERA and choice belong to women's professional and political networks and organizations. They are far more likely to participate in public spheres of politics and work.

The locally oriented anti-ERA antiabortion women are recruited from the private sphere through church, community, and neighborhood relationships. These relationships provide the ideological predisposition for antifeminism. However, Himmelstein points out that the political opinions of the pro's and anti's of abortion and ERA cannot readily be placed in liberal or political camps. In fact, antiabortion activists are more liberal than the population in general on issues such as capital punishment, U.S. intervention in foreign countries, and civil liberties. In the U.S. population, opposition toward abortion and ERA does not seem to be tied strongly to any particular range of political and economic attitudes; rather, these views seem to be closely associated with views about the family and about personal morality. Abortion, especially, correlates most directly with a conservatism on personal morality issues. Common to this conservative position is opposition to too much individual autonomy. Conservatism is focused on the need for constraints, limits, and controls on "human drives within the intimate sphere of life . . . is a concern for protecting the coherence of the private sphere against the corrosive effects of individuation."[6]

It is important to note that the anti-ERA and antiabortion women stand firmly behind policies that would provide greater equality for women in terms of equal pay, women holding public office, women in the professions, and the like. What they oppose are proposals that they perceive as assaulting the division of labor of the genders in traditional terms. They seek to protect the unity and autonomy of the family and to reject policies that would subvert the traditional role of women. "In short, [they] accept a greater role for women in work and politics, but refuse any correlative changes in women's role in the family."[7]

Himmelstein found that an analysis of antifeminist writings revealed a sense of female vulnerability where women live in a dangerous male-dominated world, where their only protection is the family, and where their relations with other women emerge from family and community ties. Theirs is not a perception of dependence on men. They see themselves as holding power and independence through their relationships to resources and support from other women in family and kinship circles.

Let me put it bluntly: These women know that the man in their lives, if there is one, can die or run off. If he does, what happens to them? With the $6,000 to $8,000 she makes and the $10,000 to $15,000 he makes, they can make it. What happens when he is gone? Where is her support of last resort? She believes that it is in the traditional family structure and, especially, in the women therein.

Himmelstein noted that this view of the world and of the importance of family networks for the independence of women did not necessarily reflect their individual situation. In fact, the impact of ERA or abortion legislation on the individual's personal situation had minor effects on their views about policy and voting. The immediate self-interest of a woman was not as important in the development of her political attitudes as certain long-standing values about society and polity and their perception of society itself. Voting was most influenced by their interpretation of the collective self-interest of the society.[8]

The point here is that the approach to meaning of women who

oppose ERA and abortion resides in their perception of the importance of the survival of the traditional family and the subsequent female independence so crucially related to it. One cannot help but wonder how the position of such women would be affected if ERA and abortion were addressed through justifications that took with the utmost seriousness the value of the traditional family and the role of kinship networks in supporting women on the cultural right.

Conventional morality is held because it is perceived to be in the collective self-interest of women and the family in society in a world they find to be dangerous and male-dominated. For these women fear that too much individual autonomy could threaten the systems of kinship on which they see themselves in such dependence. Not to see the function of conventional morality when struggling with such constraints is to miss the lived everydayness of the cultural right. While one may observe that they are basically contented with their lives, this is testimony to their courage and the strength of their relationships. It is not a sign of the absence of strife or insensitivity to the very real threat that is always just one step away.

That is not to say that all conventional morality is constructively functional. It is not. At the same time, if one splits hairs in such discussions, the sorting out often becomes abstract and disconnected from lived reality. Nevertheless, critique is required because conventional morality can also be powerfully controlling. There really can be no doubt about the way men, especially, have used conventional morality to control women, meanwhile securing for themselves a double standard in the underbelly of social life while professing motherhood, morals, marriage, and monogamy in their public ideology.

In these remarks on conventional morality it is, at least, not my intention to provide some carefully camouflaged back door of support for patriarchy. Rather, I want to maintain that such abuse can be effectively named and exorcised on the cultural right by turning conventional morality—or, really, the importance of the relationships and the struggle—into a heavily realistic critique of life as it is, of abuse as it is, of the contradiction as it is, and of new possibilities as they can be. Support for ERA, for choice, for equality, can be marshaled and sustained by a liberative and transformative interpretation of conventional morality. What won't work is the individualism, the autonomy, and the relativism of career-oriented people in management and the professions.

More than that, this does not mean that one ignores complicated issues in ethics where there really are conflicting values and claims. What must happen, however, is that such abstract ways of putting the question be given names and faces and that the relationship of morals to economic stringency be faced in dollars and cents and in the concrete struggle so many cultural-right people have in making life work.

Such an approach to ethics can deal powerfully with systemic issues as well, but not in cosmopolitan language such as "systems, structures, and consciousness." Rather, one must be concrete locally and relationally extended nationally and globally. When a woman or a man loses a job, it is not terribly helpful to talk about "the growing centralization of power in monopoly capitalism." It may help a great deal to talk by name about the board of directors of a corporation that made a decision to close a plant and what that does to families on the street, to the neighborhood or community, to one's country, and to the church. It may help a great deal to talk explicitly about where the investment is being relocated, and about what goes on *there* with families, and about whose side the U.S. government is really on, the working people here and abroad or the corporate enterprisers and their profits. Then one can make sense of substantive issues of justice that have to do with food, housing, adequate medical care, equality for women and ethnics, education for children, living-wage jobs, and a reasonable hope for the future. In this context one can ask what the *real* reasons are for the extended military presence of the United States around the globe, what it costs, whom it actually benefits, and why a loyal love of country challenges such military Keynesianism and its wealthy beneficiaries. Then the convergence of liberative traditional values and the genuinely realistic durability of conventional morality makes change urgent and breaks the ties of cultural-right people to an anesthetizing and lethal status quo.

These, then, are crucial factors in the approach to meaning of the cultural right, but we are not yet done. The place of religious belief and practice, of the meaning of faith and how it operates in relation to local realities, and the constraints on day-to-day life are of major importance in this approach to meaning. In the next chapter, we will turn to popular religion and folk theology to complete this assessment.

▶7◀

Popular Religion and Folk Theology

Seminary training in the United States basically makes people unfit to serve congregations on the cultural right, and the more a theological school sees itself as committed to the graduate study of religion, the more likely this is to be true. The reasons for this are numerous, but the basic fact is that university and seminary training is socially located in a very different place from the cultural right and operates on the basis of an approach to meaning that is as opaque to the local folk as the lifeways of the latter are uninteresting to the former. Typically, it takes five years for the average seminary graduate to "get in touch" with local people, if he or she lasts that long. Those who are more "short-lived" either quickly try another church where they find less problematic lifestyle conflicts or get out of the church altogether.

University training occurs in a context of privilege. Its interests require a life of relative leisure that provides the occasion for reflective thought, for empirical study, and for contending with an array of competing views of reality. In his fine book Robert Schreiter names such theology as "sure knowledge," an approach that aims at a critical, rational account of faith. Its use of disciplines such as reason, social sciences, and natural sciences is for the purpose of developing an exact understanding of the faith. With its focus on method (how does one know?), its rigorous analytical study, its system-building impulses, and its attempt to relate to other forms of knowledge, it is desperately important in a context where there are competing worldviews and where one must be able to render a coherent account of the faith one holds.[1]

I remember so well when I, an uninformed Bible believer, went away to Millsaps College and began to encounter the critical study of religion. At first I resisted it because it would take away my faith. I can still feel the excitement, however, when I began to see some of its rich implications. It was as though I had been in a dark building unable to discern anything very clearly when suddenly someone began to roll aside the huge doors. Then, as far as I could see, there was room to study, to discover, to search. I will never be able to repay such gifts. By the time I went to Boston University, I was wide open to its teaching, hungry to pursue what was there wherever it led.

I think now that I would not have been a Christian had I not received this kind of approach to the study of faith. It gave me an understanding of immeasurable help when I have faced the ragged edges of life as they—inevitably, it seems—come. When our older son, Steve, was killed on his motorcycle, we clearly went through the hardest time of our lives, yet I remember both the surprise and the gratitude I felt to discover that my faith was not a house of cards and did not collapse in the face of a loss I experienced as amputational. I knew it was an accident. I did not feel acrimony toward the man who ran the stop sign. I did not blame God. I did not wonder what I or someone else had done wrong or what was the source of the judgment that led to such tragedy. Gene Lowry, who preached the funeral sermon, said, "We are here by accident." At the cremation, before Shawn, Steve's brother, and I pushed him the last feet into the crematorium, Gene offered a brief statement on the text: "Shit Happens." Oh, I knew shock and denial and unspeakable grief, but my understanding of the faith received no staggering blow. All my academic life—at Millsaps, at Boston University, and at Saint Paul School of Theology—had prepared me. In the months since, I have felt a gratitude one normally withholds to all except those who save one's life.

This is my way of saying how important the academic study of religion is, and we shall return to it later; yet it is also a pursuit that misfits one, at least initially, for working with people on the cultural right. It is not that the understanding of academic theology is unimportant here; rather, it is because the social location is different and the character of understanding faith is differently formed and works with a different reality. I am convinced that academic theology can be of immense value to people on the cultural right, but not without going through a transmutation. Such a transmutation begins with an understanding of the workings of popular religion around issues of socio-psychological need, of power and powerlessness, and of spiritual hunger. Again, Schreiter informs this discussion.[2]

Popular Religion and the Cultural Right

Popular religion is the religion of the people, says Schreiter, normally the poor or the majority class or lifestyle. It does *not* mean the religion that is "in fashion."[3] In the United States it might be called the religion of the middle American, the religion of farmers, blue-collar working people, and the lower middle class. Popular religion is usually disparaged by elitists such as scholars and religious professionals. Yet Schreiter points out, significantly, that religion as a *way of life* is a good deal more than religion as a *view of life*.[4] University and seminary training tends to assume a religion that is literate, idealist, and rational, but what is required of mainline church pastors, religious leaders, and academics is a more sensitive appreciation of popular religion, rather than focusing so much on the discursive dimensions of popular religion that they miss its meaning and practice as a way of life.

This is not to suggest that one become uncritical, but that external criticism be avoided: that is, criticism that does not attempt to understand what is going on. External criticism is criticism "from the outside," which is not in touch with the people and with their needs, struggles, and aspirations.

Schreiter proposes a number of characteristics of popular religion that are especially illuminative of cultural-right religion in the United States.[5] The first of these is belief in a God who is highly providential and immediately involved in the events of the world. Certain widely heard expressions illustrate this characteristic, such as "Well, the good Lord was watching out for me today," "God sure blessed me with a quick recovery from my illness," or, in the face of the death of a child, "God just looked down and decided to take my little Jane. It's God's will. God knows what's best." Or persons often attribute divine agency to a host of unexpected benefits. "God sent this man along to fix my tire." God is directly involved in such everyday events and intervenes by providing benefits and helping people out.

Interestingly enough, while the deity is closely involved in the world, God is approached primarily through mediators. I can remember the way we talked about "Cath'liks" when I was a boy: "Them Cath-liks believe in statues; they worship those things, why, they worship Mary more than they do God." I remember the shame when I realized later that the need for such mediators arises out of the powerlessness a people experience. Powerless people feel unable to approach God directly, and the Catholics I knew were the sons and daughters of immigrants who came to America seeking an opportunity. Typically, they found a Protestant establishment that deepened their powerlessness until sufficient political organization redressed the imbalance.

Once I was teaching an elective at Saint Paul with a class of about ten people. Six of them were evangelicals. One day we were talking frankly about our perceptions, and an occasion arose in which I was able to share with them a pet peeve of mine.

"You know what bothers me? It's the way you folks pray. You always say, 'Lord, we *just* want to thank you'; 'Lord, we *just* want to say'; 'Lord, we *just* want to ask'—just, just, just, just! I get tired of that. It wears me slick. Why do you always say *just?*"

Well, when you ask for it like that, you are very likely to get it. Bob Howard, an alert and caring man who had gone through a difficult time in his life and was pulled out of it by a dramatic conversion experience, took me on.

"Tex, *just* is a word we used to express awe. We see God as highly exalted, as mysterious and beyond our reach. We don't feel comfortable approaching God in a casual or cosy way. We are hesitant to approach God, so we *just* want to thank the Lord. We don't want to take too much time, so we *just* want to say, we *just* want to thank you. You see, Tex, we don't feel that we are on equal terms with God. I suppose when you are a seminary professor, you can walk right up to God and act like a pal." (Uproarious laughter from the class.)

Since then I have been careful from time to time to use "just" in my prayers. Please, I understand that the word "just" or any other can be used in a wooden ritualism that loses the meaning it may once have held, but it is important to hear also the sense of powerlessness many people have who approach God in such a tentative way. Compassion, if nothing else, requires more sensitivity and respect than are usually accorded such religious expressions on the cultural right.

Popular religion also has a profound communal character often expressed in church suppers, enthusiastic worship services, pious associations, and religious fraternities and sodalities. These gatherings provide occasions for bonding and testimony, for developing a sense of identity and support in a world perceived as hostile and foreboding. Earlier we reviewed the research of Himmelstein on antifeminist women and their sense of the world as an evil and dangerous place. Their participation in church and in kinship networks were hedges against a world not in their control and before which they needed support.

Yet another characteristic of popular religion is a focus on devotional activities expressed in a private and personal seeking of favors, whether these be appeals to be kept healthy, petitions for special healing, deliverance from crisis, or prayers for material success. Often, religious objects call forth God's power. These can be in the form of a Bible—sometimes carried on one's person even if not read—or a cross or a religious medal.

Finally, popular religion has a complicated and sometimes humorous relationship to official religion. Directives and instructions for religious activity prescribed by official religion are ignored, and the clergy, who are appreciated very much for the purpose of dispensing blessings and presiding over basket-to-casket rites of passage, are hardly wanted at all for their admonitions and teaching about an entire range of behaviors in morality, social policy, politics, worldly decision-making, and so on. For example, studies of Jerry Falwell's Moral Majority revealed that participants in the organization agreed with Falwell religiously and certainly looked to him for his special brand of encouragement and religious justification for their lives; nevertheless, they did *not* agree with him about politics and, in fact, were deeply divided among themselves.[6] Many mainline Protestant clergy could testify to a similar disposition among their own congregants.

A number of factors stand out in this brief and limited description of popular religion that suggest some of the needs being met. The need for God's specific and immediate involvement in the world—contradicting a friend of mine who insists that God is in the wholesale but not the retail business—speaks quite directly of the powerlessness many feel, a need further specified by the use of and commitment to mediators. The perception of the world as a hostile and dangerous place provides further reason for needing God's direct intervention and for communal colonies against a world that, but for God, would be an unmitigated vale of struggle and woe.

When someone with higher education takes on these popular religious beliefs as a view of life and is insensitive to the circumstances in which this religion works as a way of life, a fundamental miscommunication occurs. More than that, theological accounts that are primarily focused on the coherence of a position will simply miss the importance of those focused on powerlessness, on belonging and security, the struggle with death, and the means for approaching a God more than adequate to the hardships they confront. Like it or not, popular religion deals with very basic human needs.

It also has serious problems. Popular religion can be false consciousness in the Marxist sense, in that adherents project fantastic illusions on reality that deflect them from their true interests, that function as an opiate and anesthetize them to basic issues of exploitation and oppression, and that misconstrue their own considerable powers to change the world into the "providence" of a supernatural God exercising an inscrutable will on the affairs of personal and collective history.[7] Also, popular religion can be idolatrous and lavish adoration on everything from plaster of Paris statues to racial groups and nation-states. Further, no one has a corner on narrow loyalties and factional strife, but certainly popular religion has one of the largest franchises. And, finally but not exhaustively, in the United States, especially, popular religion can be so thoroughly individualistic that it is unmotivated to understand and ideologically blind to corporate and systemic issues.

At the same time, it should not be forgotten that popular religion also meets *religious* needs. It cannot simply be reduced to psychological, social, cultural, or historical factors. As Schreiter points out, popular religion *is* a form of spirituality that hungers for and seeks completion in

God.[8] To miss this is to lose appreciation for the depths and subtleties in popular religion. People on the cultural right really do know pain, struggle, futility, and that creeping, desperate recognition that certain things are not likely to change at all and one must simply bear them. To suppose that people could live under such duress and not feel God's own suffering and the crucifixion at the very heart of God's reality requires one to dismiss the historical and religious experience of the great majority of the world's people.

Furthermore, Eugene Genovese points out that subaltern or proletarian religion is not merely the ideological imposition of a ruling class but can develop as an oppositional faith dedicated to the survival of its adherents.[9] Antebellum slaves, for example, could sing:

> I'm goin' home to Jesus when he comes—
> I'm goin' home to Jesus when he comes—
> I'll be waitin' at the station with my ticket in my hand,
> I'm goin' home to Jesus when he comes.

Such songs were not merely projections of other-worldly voyages in the sweet by-and-by, but rather the this-worldly anticipation of an Underground Railroad taking one from the suffocating oppression of slavery to new freedom beyond the Mason-Dixon line. Such popular religion provided the means for coping with oppression and surviving what would otherwise be an utterly devastating experience.

So ambiguity characterizes popular religion at its core. It is not to be romantically praised as some "authentic" grass-roots, mystical, populist religion of the people who live simple, less estranged folkways. Neither is it to be paternalized by those who would reduce it to the worst of its crudities as a view of life and fail to see its richer context as a way of life. Schreiter's contention that it is to be approached with respect is wise and offers a much more fruitful entrée into the faith of the cultural right.

To do theology on the cultural right will require a different theology from that of "sure knowledge," in Schreiter's language. It will require what I want to call folk theology, a theology that respects popular religion, that is able to be critical of its views *and* ways, but that does so in a form faithful to the approach to meaning of local people.

Folk Theology

Schreiter describes one type of theology as "variations on a sacred text."[10] Here the text is very important, but those using it usually operate with a metaphor different from that text, which then becomes its informing key. Such metaphors can then be greatly expanded. In our context in the United States the sacred text for the overwhelming majority of people, especially on the cultural right, is the Bible. Yet there is a variety of metaphors and expansions of these by which the Bible is interpreted and understood. For fundamentalists it is the inerrant word of God, while for evangelicals such conversion motifs as being born again—shared with fundamentalists—become the dominant metaphor. For the spiritualists in Hill's typology the dominant images will be devotional, with the use of popular passages such as the twenty-third Psalm and with metaphors where God and Christ are shepherds. Persons who hold strong ethical views will find service metaphors in the text such as "love of neighbor," "the Good Samaritan," and Christ as "the least of these." The large number of churchgoing Respectables often find commandments, rules, and proverbs to provide metaphors and images of respectability brought from the scripture to their contemporary contexts. Often these biblical sources of Respectables are heartily mixed with the wisdom of Benjamin Franklin and enduring quotations from the Declaration of Independence and Abraham Lincoln. Sometimes it is not clear to such devotees where the quotation comes from, but these quotations still have the authority and power of "sacred writ."

The point is that folk theology in the United States is profoundly biblical, and the metaphors of folk theology abound with materials from scripture. In cultural-right churches the very direct use of scripture is critical to broad acceptance by the faithful of a sermon, a program, a moral teaching, a theological belief, and, especially, a proposal for change. Also, there are some utterly ingenious rituals and instances of norm control that the faithful can use to get a "wayward"—meaning not biblical—pastor back on track. On Sunday morning after services there have been many occasions in which church members have corrected the content or the sources of my preaching or countered my evidence from the social sciences with a carefully selected verse of scripture. Sometimes they say, "Well, I wouldn't exactly call that a sermon, but I liked your *talk.*" Or, "Your sermon was good; I just like biblical preaching better." Or, more confrontationally, "Preacher, are you sure your sermon this morning squared with the Bible?" When such comments are made by enough people, they can exert considerable influence on a pastor. They become significant intrapsychic conversations on Sunday afternoon after an especially painful sermonic failure. They then set up housekeeping in the mind as one prepares next Sunday's homiletical effort.

One of the key issues in folk theology is that of identity, and it takes its own special form in the United States. Because the United States is an achievement culture, identity is hard to come by. We do not have the deep traditional ties of a society where one's identity is determined by one's family or clan. More than that, the standards for achievement (being Number One, reaching the top) are so high that few, if any, really make it in the culture's terms. One of the ways people struggle with this issue is through religious faith.

As historian Lawrence Moore has shown, the religion of outsiders often takes the form of claiming that one is the *real* insider because one is on God's side and that someday the real insiders will be in their rightful place while the "world's insiders" will be cast out.[11] An instance of such a dynamic can be found in the glee with which Jerry Falwell claimed that the mainline had become the sideline, suggesting that for him the apocalyptic dream of reversing the tables on "the unrighteous" had already begun.

Folk theology, then, has a special role in determining "who's in" and "who's out," "who's them" and "who's us." This, of course, takes different forms. For fundamentalists, it is most important that one believes the right things. Yet, fundamentalists are not of one type in terms of the implications of their views. At times Jerry Falwell seems to seek a theocracy in his political efforts, but most fundamentalists maintain a strict separation of religion and politics, fearing that the latter will corrupt the former. In their case it is important to understand that apprehension about such corruption grows out of *both* religious *and* identity concerns.

For evangelicals conversion is more important, with its interest that one be born again. Still, considerable diversity characterizes evangelicals, from those who are more conservative to those who are quite liberal in politics. Also, a large number of evangelicals divide on political issues such as defense, abortion, prayer in public schools, and civil rights. That religious faith is important to identity is clear; what form it will take in social and political implications is not clear.

Those who are more into service and devotion may not be as ideologically formed as fundamentalists and evangelicals and may be more accommodated to mainstream culture. Meanwhile, Respectable churchgoers are like deep pools under trees; they contain everything. For them respectability is itself a badge of success and bespeaks commitment to a fulfillment of the American dream, even if it is largely a compensative alternative not commensurate with the more widely sought and materially rewarded dreams of worldly achievement. There is also an authoritarian strain in some respectability that leaves its numbers prepared to force conformity on those with lifestyles different from their own. For some, keeping the boundaries clear is a passionate vocation, and they have no truck with those who would violate norms and values so closely associated with their own identities. Yet most Respectable churchgoers are more accommodated to the culture and are simply not that authoritarian. They find support for their identity where they live in kinship and friendship networks, in the church, and in the local community.

In sum, a basic dynamic in folk theology is that of establishing *who* one is, of who is "in" and who is "out." For some groups on the cultural right the identity takes on highly polarized forms, as in Jerry Falwell's attempt to "restore" America. Most fundamentalists, however, are deeply suspicious of mixing religion and politics and maintain a more separatist stance. For the great majority of those on the cultural right, respectability is the dominant form of securing cultural success, and their religious and civic identity come together in what is basically an accommodation to the culture. This stance is not typically polarized against the culture, although situationally it can be when people on the cultural right feel that someone or something represents a real threat to their way of life and, subsequently, their identity. Those who fail to understand the importance of identity in folk theology will miss one of the deepest aspects of its importance. Those who abuse this aspect can expect the wrath of the cultural right . . . and ought to.

A third aspect of folk theology is its deep communal expression. This is found in a host of forms in local churches: in worship services where close friends and neighbors gather and have gathered for years, in the cultic power of ten thousand church suppers (New England boiled dinners, wild game, frankfurters and beans, fish fries, soul food, barbecues, clambakes, Mexican food, jambalaya), in the warm friend-ships of work projects, in quilting parties and parsonage paint jobs, in bandage making for leprosy patients, and in church picnics, square dancing, cakewalks, gospel songs and spirituals, parties for the children, and memorials for those who have gone on to their reward. These are expressions of a deeply communal religious faith.

Locally oriented people tend to keep familial and friendship ties, and their churches do not simply reflect these but are constituted by them. This communal dimension is in sharp contrast to the more associational character of church life for people in the cultural middle. This means that people on the cultural right are more likely to be active participants in the church and not merely spectators, as often happens with those in the professions and management occupations. Many local people will say quite directly, "The church is my life. It's the most important thing I participate in. My family and my friends are there. We place God's church first."

This communal orientation has significant implications for min-istry. It suggests that management styles proved effective in large cor-porations or other complex organizations may simply be alien when artificially imposed on local churches and people of the cultural right. They do not operate on the basis of management by objectives, time lines, personnel, prioritization, and finalization of long-range plans. They are much more gather oriented than goal oriented, and their rituals of gathering bond them relationally. They are not nearly so much held together by some rational contract of what needs to be done as by a covenant based on identity and on local kinship and friendship ties that not only make up the church but the community as well. Such churches do not need rational managers of human resources but, rather, loving and celebrative pastors who enjoy the gathering, who can get things done with people through communal events, and who appreciate the mystery of the bonding and its special power.

This communal characteristic is closely related to another aspect of folk theology that can be described, paradoxically, as oral rather than literate and as often tacit rather than discursive. This raises the question, of course, of how something can be oral but not discursive. This is the paradox. First, by oral and not literate I do not mean that the cultural right in the United States is illiterate. It is not. There are more citizens of this country who cannot read and write than most people know, but this is not my point. I mean that folk theology tends to deal with religious faith and with the Bible in a nonlinear way that takes primarily oral expression. Perhaps the best place to see this is in the role of stories. I am intrigued by the fact that people on the cultural right, when asked to explain something, will often say, "Let me tell you a story." Then the story is told, often without the point being made, because the story *is* the point. I once asked a cultural-right eighty-year-old what it was like to get old.

"Well, the best one I ever heard on that came from old man Herbert Johnson when he was in his nineties. People said he was older than dirt and could remember when Heck was a pup. I was a kid at the time, and I asked him the same question. He said, 'Well, it's pitiful we ain't like horses. When *they* lose their teeth, they *shoot* them.'"

Folk theology operates in much the same way. An understanding of the faith is often best captured in a story. People on the cultural right are less likely to engage in conceptual refinement of ideas; in fact, they tend to distrust theorizing. One of the ways of dismissing academic theology is by describing it as "a bunch of theories." Folk theology will make much use of biblical stories and of the parables of Jesus. These provide the keys for understanding the faith.

This oral characteristic is also the reason why some churches—and more need to—make so much use of testimony. It gives the chance to tell *their* story.

Too much has been made of the abuses of testimonies by people who never do it. I remember once listening to a man engaged in an intense diatribe against testimonies, capping his own by describing some illiterate, ignorant man who got up every Sunday and told the same old story. As he was laughing at his depiction of such a silly tradition, someone in the group asked him which church he had attended where he had witnessed such goings-on.

"Oh, I've never been to a place like that in my whole life. Why, I wouldn't. I've just heard the stories."

Obviously, abuse occurs, but the people who find testimonies to be important to their expression of the faith seem far less often offended. One group where telling one's story has enormous power is Alcoholics Anonymous. There the stories are told, and some, of course, get better with each telling, but there is hardly a more healing setting for people caught in such devastating bondage. This approach of AA helps people from quite diverse lifestyles. I am struck by how often cultural-right people find in AA the day-by-day way to stay sober.

Because of the importance of oral expression, the sermon is of central importance in the worship of people on the cultural right; they still turn out to hear the word preached. Some today make the case that the sermon is passing in importance. Whether this is so in parts of the society is not yet clear. It is certainly not true on the cultural right.

With this kind of orientation on oral communication and expression, what does it mean to say that folk theology is more tacit than discursive? There is the distrust of "theorizing" already mentioned, but this is only part of the matter. For people on the cultural right, faith is a matter of the heart, and the heart knows things too deep for words. For people whose jobs and work do not usually require a lot of rational, linear, sequential communication in conceptual or written form, one can understand why religious faith would not be approached in such a way. I am struck by the way in which cultural-right people can be talking about their faith, usually in a story about their own experience, and will conclude with a comment like: "And you know, I just had this warm feeling, the sense that God was with me. Have you had an experience like that? If you have, you know what I mean." This kind of understanding can be acknowledged by the other party with a nod of the head or simply, "Yes, I know." A theology that explains things does not seem to be as important as a tacit, unstated understanding that seems to be mutually confirmed by others. A story can stir such understanding, and a proverb—not substantiated on its own terms—can express a range of nonverbal meanings that reside unexplicated in the heart of the believer.

So this faith is oral in expression in contrast to that of linear exposition, and yet it is tacit, not discursive, in the depths of its meaning. A story can suddenly call forth tacit confirmation; it does not "explain" it. A good story on the cultural right does not so much expound the faith as to evoke what the heart already knows.

Believing and Feeling

Yoshio Fukuyama some years back made a distinction between working-class and middle-class religious expression. Working-class people tend to "believe and feel" their religion, and the middle class tends to "think and do" theirs. It is an important distinction, and, while some on the cultural right will be more middle class in expression, it is worth underlining this believing and feeling characteristic.[12]

The believing aspect is related to the oral characteristic just mentioned. The concern, again, is not so much with explanation as with believing. The latter has an integrity about it. It is where people really are in terms of where they are in their hearts. For the cultural right, one's disposition, one's basic commitments, and the genuineness with which these are believed and practiced are what are really important. At the base here is a distrust of anyone's point of view being finally correct; people know that expert opinion is always divided on something that is really important. Even fundamentalists do not see themselves as buying into a human view of the Bible. They want to read it word for word and believe it as it is written. Otherwise, in their view, one is simply listening to human opinion. Most people on the cultural right will tell you that it is not finally important what someone *thinks* about the faith but whether one *believes*.[13]

Feeling, of course, is one way of determining the authenticity of a person's belief. If someone believes something, he or she will *feel* it. Genuine belief and emotional expression are closely tied. Partly, too, this is a response to the bland formality of worship that cultural-right people find in so many status churches inhabited by successful management and professional people.

Pastors who ignore this believing and feeling dimension of folk theology will be dismissed by telling comments, if one will but hear them. "Well, our preacher is a good man and very smart, but he talks a little over our heads." "Our pastor doesn't preach; she tends to do a lecture instead of a sermon."

Conclusion

What, then, is the approach to meaning of the cultural right? It is first of all a complex interplay of traditional values, conventional morality, popular religion, and folk theology. To speak their language requires a sensitive working within these frameworks that reflects the significant relationships and concrete circumstances of their lives. Their understanding of meaning begins in the closest relationships with respect to a given issue or circumstance and works the implications of that in terms of the constraints imposed by low to moderate financial resources and the relative power and powerlessness of the person or group in question. For example, the matter of abortion and the ERA for the antifeminist women whom Himmelstein studied was an issue for them that dealt directly with their kinship networks with families and particularly other women. While their views were formed not so much on their direct personal situation as on the perceived situation of women generally in those circumstances, nevertheless their critical concerns moved back and forth between these family network relationships and what they perceived as a dangerous world in terms of the financial resources and power of women. Conventional morality, meanwhile, resisted what they perceived to be the individualism, the relativism, and the autonomy that would have left them naked and alone in the face of marriage or family crisis. While Himmelstein does not discuss the popular religion of these women, one can reasonably conjecture that God was immediately provident, that mediators were significant, and that the communal dimension of their religious faith found concrete expression in their local churches and kinship circles. In the midst of all of this was a folk theology engaged in believing and feeling, biblically supported, wherein they found a tacit understanding of how one is to live in a hard world with the help of a mighty God who will finally vindicate their faithful and deeply felt conviction and practice.

This is the kind of operative approach to meaning by which cultural-right people make do with a world they cannot alter. Those outside the cultural right who care, who seek a more emancipatory society, and who want to do ministry will need to understand this way of life and meaning. Failing to do so simply excludes such persons from genuine participation in the lives of local people and from the key legitimative tools for transforming the hard edges of a tough, recalcitrant social reality.

Thus far, we have dealt with the lifestyles of the cultural left and right, but we have not examined those of the successful business and professional people of the United States. They constitute a significant group in mainline churches and provide key leadership. We turn to them in Part Four.

▸Part Four◂

The Cultural Middle

▶8◀

The Cultural Middle and the Commitment to Career

Raised in an affluent middle-class attorney's family in Kansas City, Joe Bethea left the suburban home of his parents to attend the University of Missouri. His plans to enter law school were interrupted the summer after his sophomore year, while he was working a temporary job in a small plant owned by a friend of his father. He got turned on to the idea of running his own company. Changing his major to business administration and going on to do an MBA at Ohio State, he went to work as a mid-level executive in a production company in St. Louis. After ten years and several promotions he made the plunge and began his own business. Now quite successful and in his fifties, he finds himself looking for more time with his spouse and his family, looking in his private life for a chance to "do some living" that the pressure of business and career left undone. He is successful, but he sees the horizon of his business future. Now he thinks about some other, fuller expression of himself and his family. The world of work no longer holds the excitement it once did, partly because he is not going to make it to the very top but also because other dimensions of himself have not been voiced or embodied. He yearns to be and to belong in ways that all his doings of the past did not adequately release. Making it through the middle-age crazies without divorce and without going through a major career crisis, he now shifts from a utilitarian individualism to one more expressive, one more committed to family, one aimed at a more sensitive appreciation of life in the remaining years of his business career.

Joe's wife, Kathy, welcomes this shift in Joe's interest. Throughout his career, since they met in college, she has backed him fully. Her own needs, values, and goals have been translated into his. The business and Joe's work in it have come first for her, along with raising their children. The two oldest graduated from college, and Joe, Jr., *will*, she believes, but right now he is a ski buff in Breckenridge, Colorado. Clearly a postmaterialist, he works at odd jobs that enable him to live and ski. He's only twenty-five, and Kathy says with some concealed anxiety that he still has plenty of time. All her married life Kathy has yearned for more time with her husband, and lately Joe has become more of a companion and is opening up a part of himself that Kathy knew was there but that is only now coming to the forefront in their relationship. These are the years she has waited for all her wedded life.

Jane Dewhurst grew up in a family that eked a living from a poor farm in Kentucky. Doing well in high school, she got a scholarship to the university. Later, with a master's degree in marketing, she started in an advertising company in Philadelphia and now holds a position in the upper end of the firm's management team. At thirty-five she is quite successful for her age and looks forward to a future with continued advancement in responsibility and earnings. Jane has never married, partly because she did not have time to develop a relationship requiring that kind of commitment, but mostly because she feels she never met a man who would make her career as important as his own. Her experience with dual-career couples is that the woman continually sacrifices her work in behalf of her husband. She wishes she had a deeply committed, mutual marriage and children, but that does not seem to have a place in her life right now.[1]

Jim Dubs grew up deeply impressed with the successful business and professional people he knew in his hometown. All his life he wanted to be like them. His father had finished college and worked in a garment factory in middle management. When Jim finished high school, he decided to attend a local community college, figuring he could finish up at state. After completing his A.A., he knew he wanted to go into sales and did not see any reason for further pursuit of education. Besides, he wanted to get going. Now at thirty years of age and working as a manufacturer's representative he brings home a little over twenty thousand a year, but he just cannot understand where all the money goes. Because he likes to dress nicely and feels "it's good for business," and because of his love for sports cars—notably a red ZX300—he has not been able to buy a house. Instead, he lives in a two-bedroom apartment in a fashionable complex "where all the upcoming young professionals live." Constantly in debt, Jim keeps hoping for the big break that will provide him with access to the income and position for which he so vigorously strives. Divorced, he sees several women but does not contemplate marriage for a while. "I can't afford it, and besides I rather enjoy the single life." In spite of his upbeat personality Jim hides no little resentment that life has not gone more his way. Even though he works for a large company, he does not trust the corporate world and even less the government. Often with a customer he finds himself sitting on his feelings to avoid an angry outburst that would spoil the deal.

He wants success but does not really have faith in the system that promotes it.

Herb Thames is older than Jim Dubs, and, while a bit more successful, his achievements in his career cannot match those of Joe Bethea or Jane Dewhurst. Somehow, it just never quite happened. Moreover, he sees himself as having struggled a great deal to manage both family and career. To him, more successful people have been able to provide so much better for their families that their careers seem to fit together better with their personal lives. For Herb the claims of his career and the needs of his family are often in conflict. He works hard both at work and at home, but it does not seem to pay off for him the way it does for many more successful people.

Career

One should not miss in these accounts the emphasis on career, a dominant focus in the cultural middle that sets it off sharply from the more traditional local folkways of the cultural right and the more ascendant seeking of self-fulfillment on the cultural left. The people of the cultural middle are the most successful in the society, or at least they strive to be. Career is therefore central to their lives and the major source of high social status.

Higher education is often required for top business and professional jobs, and the university or college is the place where one picks up not only the knowledge and skill but the tastes and savoir faire necessary for upward mobility. Motivation for schooling characterizes most in the cultural middle and becomes a key focus of their family lives, especially in the socialization of children.

Achievement becomes a driving goal for cultural-middle business and professional persons. One's life is so aimed and hence becomes profoundly future-oriented: planning for one's dreams, thinking about one's present job in terms of its options for promotion to another, putting off gratification in the present for the sake of long-term career and achievement gains. It is here that most women translate their own goals and needs into those of their husband, sacrificing their own aspirations for his career.

Work satisfaction for successful people in the cultural middle is high; in fact, a Gallup survey revealed that professionals and business executives "consistently report the greatest degree of satisfaction of all respondents" in "their levels of satisfaction with their standards of living, work, family income, and perceived future."[2] Their jobs are typically the best in the society with more freedom, more authority, and more opportunity to consider options and make choices among them. With this comes a strong sense of psychological well-being and self-esteem.

Business and professional careerists consistently report less alienation, more security, and less anxiety about status than less privileged U.S. citizens.

Yet all is not well in the cultural middle. With achievement expectations so high, trouble lurks beneath the surface when career aims face seemingly intractable barriers. When one finds success, the economic and the psychological benefits are high; but, equally so, problems in the career bring inordinate stress. Pearlin and Kohn found that trouble at work looms much larger for upper-middle-class men than for skilled and unskilled workers. Nearly one third of upper-middle-class men reported their biggest problems as job-related, whereas only one fifth of blue-collar men did.[3]

Individualism is alive and well in the cultural middle and is of at least two kinds. The first, utilitarian individualism, has deep roots in U.S. experience and focuses ambitiously on career, achievement, and advancement. Pragmatic and sometimes tunnel-visioned, it seeks the shortest distance between two points, the most efficient and direct means available. So instrumental in orientation, the danger of this kind of individualism is a self that becomes truncated and unemployed because so much of the territory of the psyche is left unused. The rich ranges of the self can be lost in a striving after career. The symptoms are displayed in drug abuse, suicide, family distress, and so on.

Such problems and the conformist practices of their parents led many baby boomers to seek a second and different form of expressive individualism as a way of avoiding self-loss and living out a more self-fulfilled life. More typical of the cultural left, this form of individualism nevertheless influenced some business and professional careerists, especially those on the left side of the middle. With them a tension is developing between an instrumental and an expressive individualism, a tension between career and "the good life." This tension can be graphically seen in the cultural-middle baby boomers the mass media labeled "yuppies." Constituting only 4 to 6 percent of their generation, they have received an enormous amount of media attention, some of it comical, but they do symbolize and embody the tension. Besides them, however, others feel the effect of this individualistic expression. I think immediately of the $20,000+ conversion vans driven by people in their seventies who have a bumper sticker that reads, WE ARE SPENDING OUR CHILDREN'S INHERITANCE.

Or I think of one fifty-year-old going on thirty. His hair, unblemished by gray, kept its dark hue by virtue of some color shampoo akin to walnut stain. Very successful and deeply tanned at the fitness center, he wore an expensive gold chain. The latter glittered in sharp contrast to his brown chest, revealed prominently by a "California shirt" unbuttoned almost to his navel, in spite of the fact that it was bitterly cold outside. He told me he was doing all right, but.

"My income is now a hundred thousand a year, but, you know, my problem is that I was born twenty-five years too soon. I really ought to be in this younger generation. I just missed so much. . . . I've been too busy. These younger people know how to live."

The impact of expressive individualism does not, of course, always take gaudy—and funny or sad—forms. Arnold Mitchell reports a relatively small group of Americans in the United States whom he calls "Integrateds" who are attempting to combine values of inner-directed and outer-directed lifestyles and of self-denial and self-fulfillment. Numbering only about 3 million, they seek high achievement in career, but they are also deeply interested in society and its well-being. As both "makers and movers, observers and creators, they are open, self-assured, self-expressive and often possessed of a global perspective."[4]

The Successful Winners, Strivers, and the Conflicted

At least three subgroups can be found within the cultural middle. While all three are deeply committed to achievement and career, their lifestyles are different. I will call them the Successful, the Strivers, and the Conflicted.

The Successful are upper-middle-class and business and professional people in the society. Constituting some 37 million persons, they are described by Arnold Mitchell as "diverse, gifted, hard-working, self-reliant, successful, and happy." As business executives, lawyers, physicians, scientists, politicians, and so forth, they "live the comfortable, affluent, affable, outer-directed life. . . . In the United States they tend to be 'middle-aged,' 'prosperous,' 'materialistic,' and 'builders of the American dream.'"[5]

Their average household income and assets are the highest of any lifestyle group. One fifth of these Successfuls—Mitchell calls them "Achievers"—are self-employed, and nearly half are suburban residents. While their average age is in the early forties, a very wide range of ages is represented in this average.

In the VALS research more than 95 percent of Successfuls are white, and only 2 percent are black, a major underrepresentation. It should be noted that blacks, in general, are underrepresented in the sample as only 5 percent of the total while measuring roughly 12 percent of the nation's population.[6] Forty percent of Mitchell's Achievers are women, a significant underrepresentation. If the Achiever group were ranked in terms of income and position, even further exclusion of ethnics and women would be found at the top.

A second subgroup of the cultural middle can be called Strivers because of their intense efforts to make it to the top and be like the Successful. Mitchell calls these Strivers "Emulators" and reports that they are "intensely striving people." Deeply affected by the lifestyle and values of Successfuls, they are the most outer-directed group in the United States.

"Whether man or woman, they tend to be ambitious, competitive, ostentatious, unsubtle, 'macho.'" They work hard, find themselves in concert with the trends of the times, and have a mean income below that of the nation. As oriented as they are to the life of career and achievement, they really do not understand their Successful models. They overspend and are typically in debt. Also, the occupations and training of the Strivers are different. They hold a far lower proportion of professional and technical jobs than the Successful (9 percent vs. 29 percent) and of managerial and administrative positions (6 percent vs. 17 percent). More likely to attend technical school than those of any other lifestyle, they have an unusually large number of persons with only a year or two of college, in spite of the fact that the fathers of Strivers have a "surprisingly high" level of educational attainment.[7]

Blacks and Hispanics are overrepresented in the Striver lifestyle. Thirteen percent of the Striver group were black, and 6 percent were Hispanic, exceeding their representation in the total sample of 5 percent and 3 percent respectively.[8] Mitchell sees this group as "a key resting place for many upwardly mobile members of minority groups."[9]

Like Jim Dubs in the introduction of this chapter, Strivers suffer from some basic flaws in their lifestyles, profiled in Mitchell's interpretation of the data, that will tend to keep them—at least most of them—from Successful status. Angry toward and mistrusting the establishment, "unable, or unwilling, to realign their goals," rejection prone, possessed of a poor self-image, feeling left out, low in self-confidence, unsatisfied by work or friends, and among the lowest in their assessment of personal happiness, they are driven, Mitchell believes, by their "blind upward striving" into a world of illusion and of deception designed to provide a false image to others. They tend to be "operators" and to embrace conspicuous consumption, follow the voguish fashion, and spend only where it shows."[10] Imitative and hollow, this lifestyle is in Mitchell's view debilitating, and those who move on to the Successfuls group will be a minority of the Strivers.

The third group in the cultural middle is the Conflicted, so named because they, like Herb Thames, are caught in a commitment, on the one hand, to achievement and career and, on the other, to family. The problem is that their achievement does not provide sufficient resources for surmounting this conflict.

Typically, they have much less control of their work environments and of their schedules. They are a step or two or three removed from centers of decision-making, and they lack the autonomy, the social mobility, and often the higher levels of education necessary to make it to the top.[11]

In terms of stratification the Conflicted are middle-middle class. To use a spatial metaphor, they fall between the Successful and the Respectables. Some of them, in time, let go of their dreams and become Respectables, even as a smaller number may struggle into the ranks of the Successful. The ranks of the Conflicted are likely to be home for many of the Strivers as they grow older, except for those who become Respectables and those few who make it into the upper middle class. Meanwhile, their families dream of more and make do with less. The pressures of career exacerbate those of family and vice versa. It is a conflicted life, constituted of too many claims and too few resources.

These three subgroups make up the cultural middle as I have defined it because of their commitment to career and achievement. As we have seen, they are not alike in what they think and do about this commitment, but the commitment is nonetheless real.

Family

With the focus on career and high mobility—both geographical and upward—upper-middle-class families tend to be uprooted, hence removed from kin and previous residences. They therefore place weight on the nuclear family. Companionship in marriage takes on significant importance, and the relationship is based on shared interests and perspectives. The choice of a spouse commonly takes place on a college campus, where the individuals choose someone with similar values and psychological and social compatibility. The previous class background of a person does not seem to be as important in upper-middle-class mate selection as in that of the upper class, since a college education prepares one to enter and function in the business and professional world.

With the commitment to companionship one might guess that the relationship between husband and wife would be an equal one. While an egalitarian norm of sorts has emerged in the United States, research nevertheless tends to reveal that "the husband's authority increases with his occupational prestige."[12]

Given the greater income, resources, position, and prestige of the husband, he will typically be the more powerful of the two in the family. If the wife works outside the home and has commensurate formal education and occupational prestige, the husband's power will be less.

Women who are college graduates are more likely to be employed for pay, with 60 percent of them in the labor force working mainly in professional and technical occupations. With jobs that pay well and have high occupational prestige, these women still make considerably less than the men so that, while the husband's dominance can be moderate, it cannot be erased even when the two have similar schooling and occupations.[13]

For the wife who works in the home, her principal tasks are to back up her spouse's career pursuits and to inculcate her children with upper-middle-class values and lifestyles. Subsequent research supports the findings of William H. Whyte in 1951 that "corporate wives" of junior and middle-level executives are to be highly adaptable, gregarious, accepting of the husband's commitment to the corporation, able to relate to the local community, and gracious hosts. She must *not* complain about his work load and hours or protest transfers and subsequent family moves, and she must certainly not engage in controversial activity. Her task is to keep things on an even keel for him, to maintain the home as a sanctuary, to be a good listener and an ego-soother, and to revitalize him for the next day's work. While expected to be a good listener, she really is not a part of her husband's workaday world. The husband wants her readiness to listen but not her advice.[14]

Kantner's work found three phases in the corporate wife's relation to her husband's career. The first is the "technical phase," when the husband is on the lower levels of corporate management. In this phase she is excluded from his work. In response she either (1) begins a career of her own like her husband's, which leads to greater sharing of common interests, or (2) builds barriers around the home and children, a kind of protection of her turf in reaction to being shut out from his career.

The "managerial phase" is next, coming with the husband's rise in the corporate world and the putting aside of old friendships with those whose rank in the company is no longer commensurate with the husband's. In this stage friendships are surface relationships within the corporation, and the wives feel especially lonely.

In the third or "institutional" phase, when the husband is near or at the top of the corporation, the problem for the wife is one of managing the public character of their personal lives and friendships. Work and leisure grow together so that play and friendship and corporate interest become one. "People entertain one another on yachts or over long lavish lunches—all in an attempt to mutually obligate, to create personal relations that will give someone an inside track when it comes to more formal negotiations."[15] In this phase wives are usually expected to put aside their own personal convictions, knowledge, and awareness for the sake of their public role.

Beth Vanfossen observes that "the role conflict implicit in these discussions of the upper-middle-class wife's role is presaged at the dating-mating period, when expectations of the career-oriented male that a compatible mate be intelligent, compassionate, and well-educated conflict with his expectation that her career ambitions and her own needs should not interfere with his."[16]

An additional struggle is that of the husband's being able to carry the demands of both career and family. One study revealed that those husbands able to do both, whatever the wife's career focus, had the "happiest" of the high-income families, while those where the husband's focus was too solitarily on career were the least happy.

In the socialization of children, education and achievement take on enormous importance. College education is not only assumed but continually drummed into the minds of their children. While schooling reinforces this, the child participates in a wide array of organizations such as Scouts, Camp Fire, extracurricular events and activities at school, and athletics. In these are learned important social skills and personal adjustment, not to mention organizational savvy and the capacity to manage and control people. Education is the primary means by which business and professional people can pass on their status to their children. It provides the credentials necessary for a life of career and privilege.

The affluent child also learns the importance of "achievement-in-isolation," an important first step in an orientation where relationships to people will need to be subordinated to career and its economic goals. In such children creativity, self-expression, personal growth and development, and the fulfillment of one's potential are key values in their training and socialization.[17]

Obviously Strivers do not participate fully in the patterns of the more prestigious Successfuls with better income and educations. Strivers struggle more with the tension between career and family because of their striving on the one hand and their restricted resources on the other. Constantly in debt, their marriages reflect the difficulties brought on by financial pressure. By being younger, their children are not yet in the difficult teen years for the most part, but the children do see the contrast between the status image so faithfully created yet so desperately denied by reality. Such contradictions trigger reaction, the pattern of which is not yet clear. Strivers are in a transitional lifestyle. Some of them doubtlessly will move later into the Successful group, but for most their fate is set by training, by resources, and, perhaps in part, by their own style. The future for them is one of frustration in career aims and with it either a compensative lifestyle, cynicism, or despair.

The Conflicted are oriented around the nuclear family, as are the Successful. But whereas the latter are adult-centered—able as they are to attend to the needs of the children and still pursue careers—the Conflicted are caught between being child-centered and adult-centered without being able to do either effectively. The Conflicted lifestyle is finally one of ambiguity. They are in between the Successfuls of the upper middle class and the Respectables of the lower middle class. The former are more cosmopolitan and participate in more formalized social and community affairs. The latter are more ascetic, socio-morally conservative, local-community oriented, respectable, and hardworking. The Conflicted are a strange mixture of the two. Furthermore, the material circumstances of their lives, their ideological commitment to success and family, and their mixed role in economic life of both receiving and giving orders contribute powerfully to the ambiguity of their experience. That it is an unrelieved ambiguity, given the improbability of escaping their discordant position, they must instead endure . . . and get used to it.

Politics

As one might expect, given their privilege and status, the Successful are "staunchly" Republican (58 percent) and even more conservative (66 percent). Only 19 percent are Democrats, with 24 percent Independent. An even smaller number (8 percent) are liberal.[18] They are also socially conservative—in fact, more so than any other lifestyle except Respectables. They are less likely to support sex outside marriage, "working women as also being good mothers, the legalization of marijuana, or pollution as a world danger."[19]

These findings are supported by previous research on the politics of upper-middle-class business executives and professionals. Generally they favor a laissez-faire governmental role in the economy, anticommunism, and "minimal domestic welfare." They oppose a minimum standard of living and guaranteed medical care and are anxious about the growing power of the government. Yet they *do* take more liberal positions on civil liberties and civil rights, a pattern documented as early as 1955 by Stouffer.[20]

A minority of these upper-middle-class people are more liberal, mainly a group of intellectuals that includes a good many in educational, literary, and artistic networks who often take up leadership positions in social and political movements and organizations aimed at radical social change.[21]

Herbert Gans made another distinction between "liberal-professionals," on the one hand, and "conservative-managerial," on the other. The former are more involved in professions such as education, social work, and other helping, community-centered professions. Gans found them to be active in the community, interested in good schools, better race relations, mental health, community planning, and the like. Much more cosmopolitan than the conservative managerial group, they were "more sensitive to 'ideas' in the abstract and to national issues." The conservative-managerial, on the other hand, typically came from Protestant origins and, being more business related, worked for lower taxes and stood against the liberalism that seemed to accompany the cosmopolitanism of the liberal-professionals. These professionals were also more likely to pursue "high culture": plays, concerts, museums, lectures, art shows, and performances by nationally known figures. The business group spent more time on golf and the country club, which were avoided by the professionals.[22]

An interesting shift occurs from the more typical conservative pattern of Successfuls when the focus is on the Strivers. Almost half of them (48 percent) are Democrats, with only 13 percent being Republican and 39 percent Independent. A fourth of them are conservative while 29 percent are liberal and nearly half (46 percent) are middle-of-the-road.[23] They tend to follow the fashionable trends and basically support the status quo in spite of some anger and resentment about the "establishment." Distrustful of people and institutions, they place little confidence in people who hold elective office and in the executive leadership of companies. Strivers do not regard government, public utilities, or oil companies as credible sources of information about energy issues. Their primary interests, however, are with "making it" and "getting to the top."

Politically, the Conflicted tend to identify and share the political conservatism of the Successful. In spite of the differences in their social position and that of the upper middle class, the ideological commitments of most suggest that the way *out* is *up*.

Career, Individualism, and the Self

People who pursue careers carry the dominant, established ways of doing things in U.S. society. They embody the culture at its idealized "best." Actively involved in the search for success, achievement, and the state of being Number One, they have extraordinary affirmation of their effort at every hand. Perhaps this is a basic source of an unease about it all, an unease that things do not really hold together, that they are not really working, and a suspicion—at least by the sensitive—that *if* they got to the top there would be nothing there.

Carrying out the ideals of a culture can be hazardous for the reason that one is then all the more subject to the truncations and contradictions of the established social world. If one is on the cultural left, the establishment itself can be blamed for all the ways self-fulfillment is frustrated and twisted, and there is justification in listening to one's own drumbeat, one's own inner gyroscope, one's own voice—choose the metaphor that says it. It is *expected* that self-fulfillment will be in conflict with the status quo. Or, if one is on the cultural right, one is embedded in local relationships and networks. Although their own lack of success in the culture's terms is an incessant experience in rituals of deference, in

advertising, in their own comparative "position" in the society, traditional structures nevertheless provide strong support and continuity. On
the cultural right, one can have roots.

In the cultural middle, career means mobility, mobility *around* and
mobility *up*. It is a life committed to moving. Hence, it is uprooted. In
fact, those who stop moving are those who top out, whether by choice or
by playing out the string. To be sure, deep friendships and relationships
can be formed in career ladders, but as long as career is the pursuit, these
will of necessity be secondary to the "right moves." While this priority
does not mean a crass disregard for people and relationships, it is simply
part of the demand of the life devoted to career. Of course, some cultural-middle people can live out their lives in one locale, being fortunate
enough to find an escalating career ladder in a city where one can move
up and put down roots at the same time. I think particularly here of
physicians and attorneys whose professional lives are lived out in a city
over a lifetime of practice, but these are not typical. Yet even here the
demands of career leave little time for relationships other than those tied
to business and profession. Others in the cultural middle *must* move,
and while friendships can be sustained long distance, they are subject to
the next promotion. As one executive said, "When the jobs come and go,
you have to move with them."

It does not take much imagination to see the role individualism
plays in this lifestyle, especially that of an instrumental or utilitarian
kind. Individualism in those who seek success at such intensity can
become tunnel-visioned so that entire territories of the self remain
"unemployed," really untouched and unmet. Rousseau wrote of the
person who was born a man and died a grocer. One could avoid his
elitism and name those who were born men and women and died
doctors, lawyers, executives, professors—and even philosophers.

Early in the nineteenth century Alexis de Tocqueville recorded this
utilitarian individualism in its unrelenting search for success and its
emptying loneliness.[24] The keen competition among career-oriented
individuals becomes an aspect of every relationship. Robert Carrigan,
before his death professor of pastoral care and counseling at Saint Paul
School of Theology, gave considerable amounts of his time to counseling. In a number of conversations he remarked how detrimental individualistic competition was to people with whom he counseled. He
observed that competition shows up in every relationship. In fact, one of
the basic problems he encountered in marriage counseling was the
competitive zeal each spouse brought to the marriage and the inability
of either one to work through conflicts and arguments because each had
to *win*. Individualistic competition finds its way even into marriage.

Carrigan was quick to notice gender differences, especially the tendencies of women to find identity in relationship and to want to translate their own goals and needs into those of others, especially those of their spouses. Yet among career-oriented women even these gender characteristics were shifted by individualistic utilitarian pursuits in business and professional structures. That such historic and deeply ingrained patterns of female socialization can be altered by life in occupations of the cultural middle is testimony to the power of the sources of this lifestyle.

There is little question that considerable loss of self occurs in career pursuits. Indeed, the rejection by the cultural left of such self-loss is basic to an explanation of their own alienation from the outer-directed, success-oriented adults who reared them. It is no surprise, then, that a good many in the cultural middle are searching for ways to combine career with a deeper self-fulfillment. Influenced by the cultural left yet still powerfully committed to career, these business and professional persons are the left side of the cultural middle. Yuppies, of course, are those baby boomers whose career orientation keeps them from being cultural left but whose generational moorings have pressed them also in the direction of individualistic expression. That they should seek such a lifestyle is understandable in terms of the contradictions of their affluence, their career ladders, and their generational interests. That they should be the subject of so much derision and satire testifies to the enduring relevance of humor to the contradiction of people and place.

Careers are demanding and engrossing. Yet they usually are so specialized that one cannot live out a full range of interests. In fact, a great deal must be pursued in the private sphere. As a result, cultural-middle people, particularly, experience a sharp public vs. private split.

The public world is the place where career is pursued. In some achiever settings careers are broadly interesting and involve the energy and ranging resources of the self, but for most they are highly specialized, so that the self is inadequately nurtured because only part of the self is met in striving and goal-oriented achievement. The self is also profoundly populated with the yearning to let go, to be, to belong. Career ladders have a way of suppressing, if not repressing, these longings and banishing them to the quiet, often unrecognized dimensions of the self.

There is perhaps no clearer expression in our society of the repression of the spirit than the placing of the spiritual hungers of the self beyond the executive office, the management of people, the boardrooms, the client and patient relationships of professionals, and the highly normed protocol of civility so that expressions of religious conviction of a specific kind in these relationships are somehow regarded as an impropriety. One learns early on that the naming of explicit religious commitments, such as the Lordship of Jesus Christ, or, as a Jew, to see one's people as the people of God, is not appropriate. To express such commitment in public settings is clearly a faux pas.

More than this, the cool rationality of the bourgeois human is one best served by avoiding nonrational mysteries and the impulses of the self for relationship and completion in God. Such interests and concerns do not fit the instrumental means-end rationalities of goal-oriented careers. While their careers consume much of even their private lives, nevertheless the private sphere is the place where many unanswered claims of the self are met—marriage and family, leisure, letting go, living without the agenda, and, of course, religious faith and expression.

Cultural-middle lifestyles, broadly conceived, obviously have many implications for the mainline churches that most of the upper middle class attend. While mainline churches are not merely reflections of the cultural middle, they are nevertheless highly accommodated to this lifestyle, as we shall see in the next chapter.

►9◄

The Cultural Middle and Mainline Churches

Max Weber observed that privileged classes will not typically be "prone to evolve the idea of salvation." Rather, religion serves to legitimate, to confirm their basic lifestyle and place in the world. For them it is not enough to be content with their prosperity and well-being; Weber argued that privileged groups seek to justify their standing as deserved and, equally, to be able to rationalize that the deserts of the less fortunate are altogether appropriate and right. The privileged seek through religion "this psychological reassurance of legitimacy." Theirs is a "theodicy of good fortune."[1]

Middle-Class Religion

Yet the religion of the privileged is more than merely a theodicy of good fortune. For one reason, some rain falls on everyone's parade. No person avoids unhappiness and the ragged edge of life altogether. Additionally, even the privileged—*especially* the privileged—inevitably compare themselves to peers and, at least from time to time, will be troubled by the comparison. A faith that simply justifies privilege cannot mend this tear in the cloak of status and achievement. However, like the religious expressions of other groups, those of the privileged are not reducible to the legitimation of class and privilege alone or to accounting for the unyielding character of life's blunting of aspiration. Their religious yearnings are also a search to fill the hungers of the spirit. As much fun as it may be to puncture the piety of the prosperous for the sake of an adequate accounting of their lifestyles, their own search for completion in God deserves attention and care.

For now, we need to look further into the relationship between privilege and religious faith. A classic statement is that of H. Richard Niebuhr in *The Social Sources of Denominationalism*. In his discussion of

113

the psychology of the middle class he names two "constant features which are reflected in its religious organizations and doctrines." The first is a highly developed individual self-consciousness. This self-consciousness results from a number of influences operative in their lives. One of these is their type of employment, where success and failure weigh so heavily on their individual shoulders. Members of the middle class hold their fate largely in their own hands. In contrast to factory workers, for example, these business people engage in activity that "isolates" them into relatively discrete units. They are on their own and rely on their own motivation, hard work, and business savvy. Moreover, their level of education is of such degree and such kind that it sharpens their sense of self. Further, since emerging historically from the struggle against feudalism the bourgeoisie has been imprinted by the philosophies of natural rights and their attendant individual liberties. These ideals and others of free enterprise and limited government mark the literature and tradition of business. It is no wonder, then, that their views attribute the events in society to the work of individuals. The most complex, systemic social forces are "explained" as the work of self-reliant individuals. The explanation is a fiction of such fantastic enormity that its credibility for them could rest only on the creation of a social world of profound historical and cultural activity, based on but not reducible to the economic forces of the modern Western world.[2]

It should be no surprise, therefore, that the religion of these prosperous business people is "intensely personal," says Niebuhr. Individual, not social, redemption; happiness in heaven, not the righteous millennial hope of the poor; a preoccupation with the problem of evil and "the task of justifying the ways of God to" humanity—these are the foci of much commercial middle-class religion. In the case of the poor their solidarity readies them with an "attitude of resignation," and they are thus able "to accept without explanation and without rebellion the common fate of pain and loss and death." But the individualism of the middle class with its personal sensitivities requires more solace and an accounting for a creation that is so unconcerned with the inexplicable fate and tragedy and death of the individual. In this context the faith of the commercial groups becomes comfort religion, one required to console "with exceptional attention and skill."[3]

The second feature of the psychology of the middle class is their "activist attitude toward life." Their occupational work involves a technology of things and a management of people. In the early development of the middle classes, especially among many of the Calvinists, to live was to labor. The conduct of business was the essence of life, and industry was the means to all achievement. Shot through this was a pragmatic efficiency, a means-end rationality, that influenced not only commerce and industry but the middle-class understandings of religion, ethics, and politics.[4]

Religious life is one of "constant activity." The life of faith is one of striving, of response to the dynamic will of God where one goes forth not in search of the fulfillment of a promise but in the completion of a task. It is a divinely ordained doing of God's will more than the acceptance of the justifying power of God's grace.

This activist approach to life views sin not as a condition but as a deed, not one where all society and nature are "infected" but as "the personal failure of the individual." Righteousness, then, is no longer faithfulness to the covenantal reality of life but right actions in obedience to the commandments of God. A code of right conduct necessarily follows from this approach, and righteousness becomes, again, an individualistic matter. The doctrine of salvation is continuous with these, being understood as "a process within the individual, not the construction of a divine kingdom." This individual change comes through conversion or education. One is not so much redeemed from sin and guilt or estrangement from God as delivered from bad habits and evil desires that war against the divine command.

The interests of the middle class also influence religious ethics. The personal virtues of "honesty, industry, sobriety, thrift, and prudence" are advanced by the very nature of economic life for the middle class, not to mention their place in the pursuit of success and the subsequent status of the individual.[5]

Family life takes on significant value in the middle class for at least three reasons. For one thing, much of the social fulfillment of the middle class takes place in the family. For another the lifestyle can provide a rich type of family experience because of its emphasis on the liberty and personal accountability of the individual. And, finally, the concern about family ethics may well be an unrecognized response to the threat individualism poses for the family. Niebuhr further suggests that this special interest in family morals may be a "natural concession" that individualism grants to "the suppressed social character of religion."[6]

Thus activism and individualism have shaped the religious ethics in profound ways. Indeed, the good itself is an individualistic one, with moral activity taking on a Deuteronomic pattern where the righteous prosper and the wicked go to ruin. Poverty, consequently, is moral failure, demonstrable proof of a lack of character, while success becomes the mantle of blessing God places on those who have the will and the energy to pursue the disciplined, orderly life. To be sure, wealth and success can be misused, as can any of God's gifts, but they are no longer objects of suspicion but proof of divine favor.

The ethic of the middle class holds undeniable strength in its heroic capacity for self-discipline, in its stringent vocation of personal responsibility, and in its attentive response to the voice of individual conscience, especially when it empowers them to stand against the authoritative dictates of church and state. But Niebuhr concludes that "this morality is incapable of developing a hopeful passion for social justice. Its martyrs die for liberty and not for fraternity and equality, its saints are patrons of individual enterprise in religion, politics and economics, not the greater benefactors of mankind or the heralds of brotherhood."[7]

Lastly, the organization of middle-class churches is permeated, as one might expect, with these characteristics of an individualistic and activist view of faith, life, ethics, and virtue that inevitably reflects the commercial and economic base of the bourgeois existence. Usually democratic in constitution, their mission is one of character-building, the preservation of morality, and obedience to divine will, individualistically conceived. Yet uncomfortable with the potential excesses of a thoroughgoing democracy, their churches will be representative in government and polity. Their leaders, democratically chosen, have the responsibility not only of teaching but of protecting the constitution of the church, a constitution composed not only of doctrine but of discipline.

Moreover, the churches of the middle class will seek organizational independence from both the economic order and the state. In the first instance it is a move of the church toward privatism and away from direct engagement with the workaday world. In the latter it is separation of church and state, one that does not merely guarantee the nonestablishment of an official church and free exercise of religion but, indeed, for many the removal of faithful *action* from the public square and the political arena.[8] Hence, the split of the public and private sphere, so pronounced in our own time, was set in place early in the development of middle-class religion.

As one looks back over this summary of Niebuhr's discussion of the psychology of the middle class, it will be apparent at a number of points that he is discussing earlier forms of bourgeois religion growing out of the Reformation and the rise of commercial classes in the West. Yet one can also find striking continuities with middle-class religion today. Obviously, individualism is alive and well, although, as we shall see, it has gone through significant change even in the past twenty-five years. The activist approach to life has not diminished. In fact, with the increasing place of career in the lives of cultural-middle Americans, it has perhaps taken on a special intensity because of the uprooted character of their lives. Middle-class religious faith continues to legitimate and confirm their basic lifestyle and status in the world. The "reassurance of legitimacy" and the "theodicy of good fortune" seem not to have attenuated. Related closely to this is the highly accommodative character of middle-class religion serving the lifestyle and lifeways of the establishment and the dominant values of the United States. Its task is often "motivational" and "inspirational," a shot in the arm to enable one to go back into the world and work hard. It does not usually raise questions about the broadly systemic character of what is being done and the way in which a church, confined primarily to the role of spiritual energizer, is contributing to a society and an ideology fundamentally alien to its gospel. Its message of grace fuels the drive to make it to the top, and sanctification is no longer being set apart for the mission of God but an accommodative life of bourgeois virtue serving efficiently in its means and, finally, unquestioning of the ends pursued.

Congregations of Civility

Churches populated by large numbers of business and professional people take on an interesting mix of individualism, privatism, pluralism, and tolerance. Roozen, McKinney, and Carroll, in their study of Hartford churches, reported on four types of "ubiquitous presence" in terms of congregational life: congregation as citizen, as activist, as sanctuary, and as evangel. The type most relevant for our consideration here is that of congregation as citizen, with strongly normed civility.[9] This is the type of church where one is most likely to find the politically conservative and culturally accommodated upper-middle-class business and professional people.

The civic congregations displayed a genuine concern for the world and a clear interest in social justice. Yet the expression of this concern was limited to consideration of education about, and analysis of, issues; only rarely did it result in direct action by the congregation. Such exploration of issues was expected and appreciated; however, it did not eventuate in corporate action.

The reason is that beliefs and ethical commitments were private matters and were considered an individual personal responsibility. In their logic of meaning a clear boundary existed between personal opinion and corporate action. The pastor and others had every right to personal opinions but should not appear to be speaking for the congregation or implicating others, either in expression of their point of view or in their actions.[10]

In one congregation Roozen et al. found a kind of "vague theological liberalism" that amounted to little more than love God and neighbor but had little consensus as to the applied meaning of this. Application is "a matter of individual responsibility and discretion." The authors see one of the problems here as the lack of a clear theological center, whether of belief or ritual observance.

The problem is also compounded by an overriding commitment of civic congregations to "tolerance and respect for diversity." Roozen et al., in fact, claim that intolerance or an attack on pluralism may be the one issue on which civic congregations could mount sufficient consensus to engage in direct action.

What is evident in civic congregations is their commitment to be good citizens and to "avoid taking stands on issues that alienate their members or the broader community."[11] Such an avoidance grows out of the pluralistic situation in U.S. society and of the kind of civil religion characterized by John Murray Cuddihy as one that demurs at specific assertions about one's faith in Christ in public settings because they are seen as a "social impropriety" on the one hand and a religious heresy on the other. Roozen et al. suggest that an additional impropriety is a congregation taking a position on an issue of some controversy.[12]

Because of the high commitment to toleration of diversity, congregations of the cultural middle will often mute public issues and focus instead on private matters such as "family life, personal growth, personal morality, and so forth."[13] Such concerns as these feed into a preoccupation with their own subjectivity and the attempt to deal with the pressures on their private lives brought on by public attention to career. The church, then, becomes the place where one faces private interests, which are important, but which can also focus the attention of the church away from the weighty public issues of the day.

Such a preoccupation promotes an additional neglect because it typically fails to see the relationship between personal pain and public ill. When the church focuses on the private sphere to the neglect of the public arena, the pervasive, implicit teaching of such a stand is that the private and the public are unrelated. Such a stance fails to see how personal the political is and how political the personal. We have known for some time, for example, that measures of family instability follow indices of economic hardship: During economic downturns divorce, Aid to Families with Dependent Children rates and other indices of "family instability" tend to go up. Unemployment is an especially powerful predictor of divorce and welfare dependency statistics. In short, family statistics are highly responsive to economic forces.[14] Moreover, in 1984 the Gallup Report, *Religion in America*, cited a Johns Hopkins study revealing that a 1 percent increase in unemployment "is accompanied by an increase of 37,000 deaths—including 27,000 fatal cardiovascular cases, 650 murders, and 920 suicides—plus 4,000 additional admissions to state mental hospitals and 3,300 more criminals sentenced to prison."[15] Gallup also reports that a major factor contributing to low self-esteem is unemployment. The public really is personal and private, and these few statistics are but the tip of a mammoth iceberg of human misery and degradation.

Churches of the cultural middle, however, are not oblivious to human need, but, rather than deal with controversy, they give their attention to human services. This attention gives vent and expression to compassion, and the contributions of churches across the land would be sorely missed should they ever cease. More than that, human needs are met and deserve a response. The problem, however, is that responding to human needs and avoiding controversial issues usually means that the causes of such needs are not engaged and dealt with and the church winds up dealing primarily with the symptoms of social maladies rather than their sources.

Why are cultural-middle people and others hesitant to approach controversy? Certainly part of the reason is the protection of privilege, and the business and professional achievers of the society are the most privileged except for the wealthy. I remember once lecturing in a local church on implications of Christian faith for justice and social action. When the session ended, a senior vice-president of a local bank approached to raise sharp questions about the content of my speech.

"Mr. Sample, the biggest problem we have in the church today are people like you pushing the church to engage in controversial issues. If clergy and seminary professors like yourself would stop pressing these things and go back to preaching personal salvation, the church would be better off and we laity could then go into the world and make the application of our beliefs and moral teaching. Leave it to the individual."

"Do you do this in the bank?"

"Of course."

"Let me ask you. As a Christian do you believe that you have a special responsibility to the poor?"

"Yes, I do. I believe I need to help them every way I can. It's my Christian responsibility."

"As a Christian are you for progressive taxes that help the poor or regressive taxes that favor the rich?"

"As a Christian I'm for progressive taxes."

"Then will you go to the bank tomorrow and order your lobbyist in Jefferson City [the capitol of Missouri] to work for progressive tax legislation?"

"That's silly! You know perfectly well I can't do that. I have to represent the interests of our depositors and investors. Why, if I did that, I wouldn't be able to keep my job. They'd have a new person in within the week."

He was, of course, correct that he could not do what I suggested. Yet his point illustrates why the mission of the church cannot be adequately fulfilled by leaving it only to the efforts of individuals. This is especially true in the case of the cultural middle, where people are caught in the cross-pressures of positions of privilege. Roozen et al.

found that members in civic congregations "acting out of an ethic of individual responsibility frequently find themselves caught between cross-pressuring interests—those of family, neighborhood, job, racial or ethnic identity, and other organizational involvements—that make it difficult for them to challenge the status quo in terms of their faith commitments."[16] In order not to put at jeopardy their affluent position by taking on the status quo, these cultural-middle careerists typically do not challenge, do not raise questions, and offer no alternative proposals in terms of their faith, so that when action is left to individual discretion nothing much happens. If the church were able to take stands as a congregation, it could offer a theological contribution not easily ignored and could do so as a community of faith and not merely as a vulnerable individual acting alone.

In summary, cultural-middle congregations made up of career-oriented people are strongly individualistic, pluralistic, highly tolerant of diversity, civic-minded, maintain a private-public split, and tend to avoid action on controversial issues. This situation grows out of the cross-pressures such people experience in positions of privilege on career ladders.

The Cultural Middle, the Clergy, and the Churches

"I have real problems with this church," he said. "There just isn't any leadership here. They are good people, you know, the salt of the earth, but I can't get them to take responsibility for things, to grab hold and take off with something. I'm ready for a move."

Jim Salsman was a forty-year-old pastor who had been an excellent student in seminary and had a keen interest in organizational development and church administration. But as the pastor of a blue-collar and lower-middle-class Respectable church in an older residential area of St. Louis, he was dying! Nothing he had learned about leadership, planning, organizing, and putting programs together had worked unless he basically told people what to do or did it himself. Although he was energetic he was worn out, not so much from work as from his conflicted frustration.

Within the year he moved to an upper-middle-class church of business executives and professionals with a membership of 750.

"Wow! This is the church I have looked for all my life. The people are wonderful. We are abundantly rich with leadership, and we talk each other's language. I can tell that they feel good about my competence, and I exult in theirs. I think I could stay here the rest of my life."

Salsman's training and lifestyle found resonance and compatibility with his Successful congregation. Schreiter reminds us that the popular religion of the middle and upper middle classes "tends to coincide with the religiosity of the clergy when it comes to the resolution of religious need."[17] I would add that similarities in education and taste, if not always in income, further fuel this compatibility. Because of their occupational training and experience Successfuls typically fill leadership roles in mainline churches, and most highly educated pastors find working with them more congruent with their own styles and interests.

In the Southern Baptist Convention (S.B.C.), a denomination not always recognized for its large number of Successfuls, a VALS study found that while over half (53 percent) of the Southern Baptists are Belongers (Respectables), nearly 29 percent are Achievers (Successfuls). They found that these Achievers are:

1. Active in their attendance
2. From medium and large-size churches
3. Attending a church a medium distance from home
4. Involved in church now to the same degree as a year ago
5. Involved as church leaders
6. Evangelistic
7. Mixed regarding personal devotional practices
8. In the middle regarding a desire for increased emphasis in certain religious areas
9. Moderate readers of religious books[18]

Moreover, a VALS study of church leadership in the S.B.C. found that 33 percent of these leaders were Achievers, as against 56 percent of Belongers. The difference in their leadership styles is especially interesting for our purposes here. The study found that they were "driving, efficient, good at the job, successful." Decisive but not rigid, smart and firm but not autocratic, they are more practically oriented and get things done, typically measuring success in terms of "production." In contrast, Belongers prove to be "conscientious and hardworking" but may not always be able to produce results. They are more "indecisive, apprehensive, and undemanding." To them affiliative concerns take priority over production, and they are most effective where personal relations are more important, where the situation is structured with clear and set rules, and where the decisions are not so important.[19]

Doubtlessly there would be variations among denominations both in the proportion of Achievers and in their religious activities, but the S.B.C. does provide one important picture of their role in the largest Protestant denomination.

The presence of upper-middle-class executives and professionals is also quite evident in a study of large United Methodist churches conducted by Warren Hartman and Robert Wilson. Professionals and executives make up 25.8 percent of the principal wage earners in that body. Clinical, technical, sales, and middle management make up another 24.3 percent, with retired persons representing the third highest percentage (22.4). Blue-collar workers, business owners, and rancher-farmers constitute 12.9, 10.9, and 2.7 percent respectively. Such data indicate that the majority of large church members came from middle and upper-middle income classes.[20]

In contrast none of the major Protestant groups are reaching Strivers. In a study of *"religious preference, not actual church membership,"* Strivers were underrepresented in all these Protestant groups, with only Roman Catholics and Greek Orthodox being overrepresented by them.[21]

The VALS study of Southern Baptists found that only 4 percent of their members were Strivers and that they are:

1. Lowest in attendance
2. From the extremely small and large churches
3. Likely not to attend where they are members
4. Less involved than they were a year ago
5. Not involved as church leaders
6. Least likely to engage in witnessing activities
7. Least likely to observe personal devotional periods
8. Unlikely to desire an increased emphasis in certain listed religious areas
9. Least likely to read religious books

In essence, they are marginally related to the church and do not seem to have strong religious commitments.[22]

Strivers fall mainly between the ages of eighteen and forty-four, so that they represent, especially, the largest group of unchurched baby boomers who would fall in the cultural middle in our typology. As such they present an important challenge to mainline churches. Numbering some 16 million people in the United States, they compose, along with cultural-left baby boomers and the poor and near-poor of the cultural right, the largest unchurched groups in the society.[23] In the next chapter, as we consider approaches to the cultural middle, Strivers will be one important focus of our attention.

▶10◀

Cultural–Middle Pain
and Explanatory
Theology

The previous two chapters have described a number of characteristics of the cultural middle that give pause for concern. First, the individualism of business and professional people not only leads to loneliness (reported as long ago as the early part of the nineteenth century) but also feeds a fictionalized view of social reality that misunderstands the corporate nature of the church and leaves cultural-middle people unequipped to grasp the systemic character of oppression and the depth and range required in social transformation.

Second, this individualism, by placing a façade over the social nature of the self, loses the sense that, while we have a centered self, we are also deeply constituted of others. Not only do "people need other people," we are, in part, *composed* of them. To miss this socially constituted character of our very selves is to anesthetize our relations to others. It can be like a saddle block used in surgery before an operation. One's legs and lower body are there, but one cannot feel them. Perhaps it is here that one finds the roots of the loss of social compassion. Let me be clear—it is not that the cultural middle lacks compassion, but rather that it lacks *social* compassion. This lack stems, I believe, dominantly from individualism.

Third, the activism, the life oriented around being *busy*, the haste and heavy attention to organizational matters at work, in the community, in the family, and at church—all these contribute to a pattern named often by the cultural middle as "the rat race." The focus on deeds and doing has its consequences in the loss of being and belonging. The truncation of the self rides concomitantly with this busyness.

Fourth, it should not be surprising that, in light of these expressions of individualism, activism, and self-loss, the cultural middle seeks such a split between the public and the private world. Their privatism is a hedge against an amputation of the self's becoming a decapitation. The utilitarian rationality of the contemporary world of career, the uprooting of geographical mobility, the distance of extended family, and the short-term networks of friends or their location around the country (and, hence, not close by) leave the cultural-middle professional or business person searching for a place to *live*, typically in the private sphere. As a result many questions of meaning, the matters of the soul, some way of giving the family a grounding in purpose that is adequate to those poignant moments of love and joy are lost because the compelling sense that life is meant to be more cannot be encompassed by empty tin-can slogans of "winning," "getting to the top," "the new entrepreneurial spirit," "the bottom line," and so forth, ad nauseam.

Finally, for now, the civility of middle-class religion falls into place. Searching in the church for a private sphere of meaning and relationship and yet cross-pressured by the constraints of career and privilege, one finds in the local congregation a place where one may examine issues that count but where the power of good etiquette sanctions against commitment that involves others and takes action on the issues of the day. Indeed, the church is reduced to a place of motivation and study but not of consequences and action. One of the problems of such church life is that it deepens the malaise of business and professional people.

It is not so much an explicit teaching as the consequence of an entire logic of participation that religious faith really has nothing to say about outcomes. All is left to the individual. It is a world where the final word is individual autonomy, relativism, subject to one's point of view. This leads not only to the paralysis of the local congregation but to a dreadful view of reality and the sinking miasma of anomie, powerlessness, and meaninglessness.

To be sure, the hunger to do something that is important and counts cannot be assuaged by civility alone, and therefore many seek satisfaction in ministries of service to relieve the symptomatic distress of deeper, systemic injustices. Yet those who are diligent in their personal lives on environmental matters, who save aluminum cans, drive economical cars, and practice an ethic of care, know that their efforts barely touch the ecological devastation of the planet, now moving in a direction that could in the near future be irreversible. Or those who struggle with issues of racial and gender justice find themselves again and again in churches that, at the most, "just talk." And those who seek peace find themselves in churches so filled with nationalism and a Manichaean view of the United States as righteous and its enemies as evil that even the ethic of civility can dissolve quickly into one either of passionate incivility or abject dismissal.

How does the church deal with the dominantly conservative,

professional, managerial, cultural middle that is career-oriented, individualistic, privatistic, and cross-pressured in its privilege and that, in its religious life, finds civility to be the central means by which it can confirm its status and standing in order to arrive at a theodicy of good fortune? Perhaps the place to look is in congregations that do not fit the civic type outlined in the last chapter.

The Activist Church

In the work of Roozen, McKinney, and Carroll on congregational presence in Hartford, one of their types was that of congregation as activist. Because churches of this type were most concerned and involved in a ministry of justice in public life and social policy, they can be instructive at this point in our discussion and can provide a model for working in the cultural middle. Several characteristics are key.

In the first place, pastoral leadership is essential in the formation of a church whose mission is profoundly concerned with social justice and the issues of the day. The pastor is "the symbolic representative of the sacred within the congregation."[1] Regarded by laity as having the special expertise required by the church and by virtue of being (often) the only full-time, paid person in what is overwhelmingly a volunteer organization, the pastor has the greatest opportunity for shaping the missional purpose of a congregation. Moreover, taking on issues brings controversy and conflict. It would be very hard for any church to take an activist stance without strong pastoral leadership and support.

Roozen et al. compared a Roman Catholic and a Baptist activist church. They found that the hierarchical polity of a Catholic parish makes it possible to effect a change in a congregation's mission orientation more quickly. They suggest that in a church with a congregational polity a change to an activist stance will come more slowly through the nurture of "lay leadership who shape the ethos and orientation of a congregation, including the selection of pastoral leadership." My experience indicates that this same pattern will be necessary even in Protestant churches with episcopal polity, both because of the strong role of lay leadership in cultural-middle churches and because of the commitment to a participative style of governance in the congregation.

A second characteristic of activist congregations was the grounding of their mission in a theology in which social justice has a definite and essential priority. I shall return to this characteristic later in the chapter to suggest an approach to theology more in keeping with the logic of meaning of the cultural middle.

Third, the activist churches in the Hartford study worked diligently to provide "pastoral care and nurture" for members of the congre-

gation. The personal needs of church members complemented the justice concerns of the church. The pastoral team of the Baptist church had
a division of labor in which the senior pastor was primarily responsible
for pastoral care and nurture and the associate gave primary attention to
community ministries. Here is a point in which the relationship of
personal pain and social ill can be named, in a context of compassion
and pastoral care. Moreover, the need for personal support and inner
renewal is crucial to avoid burnout, on the one hand, and, most basic, to
deepen one's relation to God. Roozen et al. report on a study done by
sociologists Jeffrey Hadden and Charles Longino in which an experimental congregation devoted itself to social action, specifically racial
justice, but experienced serious difficulty because there was no clear
theological mission holding the church together and the personal needs
of its members and their conflicts were ignored. Besides, it is contra-
dictory and hypocritical for a church body to champion justice and not
love and care for one another.

A fourth characteristic of these activist churches was the avail-
ability of independent resources, especially endowment, desirable rental
property, and funding, on which they were able to draw for social action
and for social services. Neither of the two activist churches had sufficient means to carry out their ministries without these resources. Roozen
et al. maintain that such resources are not, in themselves, "necessary and
sufficient conditions for an activist missional stance; nor do such
resources need always to come from the outside" or from endowment.
Nevertheless, sufficient funding has a clear, freeing effect on a congregation's ministry of justice, provided that this ministry is central to its
missional identity.

Finally, it needs to be reported that activist congregations are not
unanimous in their commitment to justice and action. Some members
want the church to be a sanctuary seeking withdrawal from the world or
pursuing there an identity in community. Others prefer a civic congregation with an educational rather than an activist approach. The church
that does not have such diverse points of view will be rare.[2]

In sum, cultural-middle congregations committed to social justice
and action will require strong pastoral leadership, a grounding in a
theology of mission where justice is a central priority, a compassionate
concern for the personal needs and pastoral care of the congregation,
and—a factor of no little importance—independent resources.

In the remainder of this chapter I want to address two of these four
characteristics in some detail. First, I want to approach personal need
and pastoral care from a perspective that places them in a systemic
context; second, I will describe the style of theology that will be most
effective in working with the cultural middle.

Personal Pain and Social Ills

People of the cultural middle have very real problems, many of which are tied rather directly to their position and lifestyle. While we certainly cannot address all of the problems confronted by professionals and managers, we will here consider those that are pervasive and that reflect deeper maladies in the society. Also, while these problems are not necessarily the special domain of the cultural middle, it is important to understand that the most successful fulfillers of the American dream are nevertheless subject to them.

The first of these, stress, is now a buzzword in society, but it names a pervasive problem, one no less troublesome for the cultural middle. The problem of stress seems to come with the territory. It is related closely to both physical and emotional problems. Thousands of articles in magazines and journals address the gravity of stress and name an endless list of antidotes to manage it. We are urged to use a host of personal and psychological medicants, including transcendental meditation, biofeedback, relaxation therapy, sleep correctives, exercise programs, medication, counseling, and religious prescriptions from "get right with God" to "be happy" attitudes. In the public discussions of stress and the suggestions for reducing it, I am struck by how infrequently it is addressed as a social or collective problem.[3] With exceptions, stress is considered to be a personal and individual difficulty, and its solution rests in the hands of each person. Social critique is virtually absent. Yet the fact of stress in the cultural middle and its pervasive effects requires a new interpretation, one more adequate to account for its systemic sources: its relation to the structure of work and the cultural beliefs and values of the United States.

One of these cultural factors is the enormous emphasis on success and achievement, especially in the cultural middle. In its most secularized form it is understood as winning. A major problem with such values is the connection they have to personal worth. One's value, one's dignity, is tied to how successful one is or can become. In the tradition of Christian thought it is a secular form of works righteousness. Worth is *made* in our culture, not *given*. It comes with effort and hustle. If it does not come, the individual has no one to blame but self. The destructive character of this cultural formation has not yet received a critique of sufficient and sustained magnitude to challenge it. Too many churches implicitly and explicitly endorse and advance it.

The other side of success in the culture is failure, a pervasive aspect of life in any setting, and one all the more sharpened in the career pursuits of the cultural middle. There may be no greater fear than that of failure among professional-managerial people. I am impressed by how failure is used in a culture so oriented toward success. The popular wisdom is that, if one has lemons, "make lemonade." Or "use your failures to help you succeed." Or "learn from your failures." Or "turn failure into success." By now, it is not surprising that these maxims are so individualistic but, rather, that such popular teaching does not deal with the devastating blow to one's dignity when failure comes to a person in a culture like ours. Advising someone to turn failure into success may indeed reverse a previous default, but a new success leaves unmet and unanswered the issue of dignity. It cannot be earned. Here, clearly, is a theological problem, one that can only be dealt with adequately in theological and spiritual terms. Yet it is also the tip of a cultural iceberg, one that needs transformation throughout.

The sharp edges of failure are experienced at least at three points by most people. One is in the experience of "topping out." One man told me that his life had been that of one promotion after another until the last ten years. "Since then," he said, "I seem to move only in a lateral direction. I've got more lateral movement than an NFL middle line-backer." He made the joke to take attention away from his own pain. In the conversation that followed even his body langauge became deferential and tentative as he talked about his "failure"—this in spite of the fact that by any objective and humane measure he was a successful man. The second point is that of mid-life crisis. Many men see here for the first time the outline of their future. How much they will advance and where they will get become reasonably clear. It is a time of reassessment and often the withering of the dreams of ambition. It can be an occasion of such aberrant behavior that we call it the middle-age crazies. For women who have placed the rearing of children and the husband's career ahead of their own, it may be a time to give career serious new thought and effort. Their struggle will now be between more time with their spouse and the outlay of energy required by a new or renewed career. Retirement is the third place where failure can be ominously present. For many their lives are "over." Advice to "redirect" is a bitter affront to those who feel they never achieved the place they had originally sought to begin with. They know in their bones that in this success culture a retired person is either a has-been or a never-was. Neither status is desired by people whose lives have been staked on career. I know one religious leader who faced mandatory retirement age terribly discontented over what he had not done and resentful of a status that he knew would make him "powerless" and confine him to a "dignitary role," as he said, "a toothless tiger munching on sawdust." He died a few years later, probably overwhelmed by honorific neglect.

These issues constitute a persistent pressure on the family. The struggle to balance the claims of career and home are endless. Ours is a culture that rewards very highly those people—mostly men, so far—

who will spend seventy to eighty hours per week away from home. These pressures mount exponentially in single-parent households. Balancing the claims of work and companionship and of career-significant activities with the needs and joys of children is incessant, and too many parents come to the end of the child-rearing years realizing that the opportunity to be with and know their children is now gone and cannot be retrieved. Moreover, while some corporations are now giving the families of their executives significant consideration in job assignments and moves, the dominant pattern is one where these considerations are secondary at best.

Most of this applies to the Successful, those with the greatest achievement and material rewards. The fate of the Strivers is far worse because of the distance between their dreams and their circumstances. Theirs is a position that encourages the construction of fictions, compensative behavior, and conspicuous consumption. In the world of their more limited opportunities, these fictions and behaviors will place even farther beyond them the goals of an overwrought ambition. As they age most will probably move to a Respectable lifestyle. A few will "make it." The danger for the others is cynicism and bitterness.

In summary, a list of the painful experiences of cultural-middle people will include stress, the struggle for dignity through achievement, failure, and pressure on the family. These are focal points of contradictions in "the good life" of the American Dream at its best. Also, each of these issues falls at a connecting point where personal pain—crucial in the individualistic U.S. psychology and especially the cultural middle—and systemic issues are joined. These are the places to raise questions about the structure of work and the organization of business and the professions in the United States. These are the places for a cultural critique of individualism and its visions of success, and these are the places where concern for family can arouse a critical searching of the ways in which personal pain is the result of social ill.

A breakthrough here could represent a significant altering of bourgeois consciousness and make possible a more sensitive reading of issues of race, class, gender, peace, and ecology. Let me be clear; even such a change is not a panacea. It is a beginning. I do not see the cultural middle as the agent of social change to bring about a transformed society, although these people participate in it. Rather, I see the cultural middle as providing the most significant leadership in the church. Some shift in their perspective is necessary if the church is to influence the direction of our culture. So my proposals are more modest. How can the church, by focusing on the pain of the cultural middle, reshape the consciousness of a major segment of its membership and the most significant group of its leaders? If the task of the church in regard to the cultural left is to reach this significant population group and to respond, especially to their social consciousness, and if the task relating to the cultural right is to develop ministry more responsive to their lifestyles and to take their just interests more seriously, the task for the cultural middle is to challenge the dominant ethos of the culture and to rouse a new religious worldview among cultural-middle church people. Such a view, more compelling than the ideologies presently in place in the wider culture, will need to be one that is explicitly Christian and that counters bourgeois mentality. The latter is severely worn and too vastly overstretched to account for the complexities of the late twentieth century.

Obviously, as important as it is to place personal problems and struggles in the larger social context, it is not enough. These matters require theological engagement. This engagement will need to take a form appropriate to cultural-middle people. As we have seen, cultural-left people respond to theology as journey, and cultural-right people understand faith in terms of a folk theology. The cultural middle can be approached from yet a third theological style.

Explanatory Theology

I was lecturing at a mental health center in Kansas on lifestyle issues. At one point in the session I mentioned Paul Tillich. During the discussion period following the presentation, a woman on the front row asked me how Paul Tillich understood heaven. Well, the question was not exactly aimed at the topic of the night, and I, wanting to respond to what was clearly a genuine interest of hers but not one I wanted to spend time on then, answered her in about two minutes—impossible— but basically I reported Tillich's view in Volume III of *Systematic Theology* where the temporal is "elevated" into the external.[4] Then I hastily went on to the next question.

After the session ended, one of my acquaintances on the staff came over to me. She was followed by an Anglo man in his mid-thirties.

"Tex, this is Dr. James [not his real name], the new psychiatrist on our staff. He wants to ask you something about Paul Tillich."

As we greeted each other, I thought to myself, He must be a Christian who wants to deal with some aspect of his own beliefs in relationship to Tillich's theology. He broke my supposition with a surprising comment.

"Tex, I have been a Hindu now for some fifteen years. While I was raised in the Christian church, I never heard Christian thought deal with reality the way Tillich apparently does. In fact, it is not dissimilar to some of my own Hindu belief. Would it be possible for me to attend classes at your school and learn more about Tillich?"

One does not usually expect such a comment in the middle of

Kansas, but increasingly it is the way the society is. Because social location so affects the way we think and the way we do theology, one should expect highly diverse religious beliefs in a society as economically differentiated and complex as that of the United States. Robert Schreiter maintains that, in a "highly specialized urban economy" where there is a "plurality of competing worldviews," thought about faith will be pressed to take the form of what he calls "theology as sure knowledge," as "scientia."[5] Such theology characterizes mainline and Roman Catholic churches in the United States and, of course, is the approach to theology found in universities and theological schools. It is also the type of theology most likely to be found among the clergy.

Theology as sure knowledge attempts to render a "critical, rational account of faith" and makes use of secular disciplines that can provide the most "exact" or "sure" knowledge, such as, reason and the natural and social sciences. Such an approach seeks to relate theology to other (competing) forms of knowledge. It does careful analysis in its work and attempts to provide a rigorous account of the faith within its own internal "theological circle," to use Tillich's phrase.[6] "Theology as sure knowledge" labors as intently on method as it does on conclusions. In a society where many points of view seek credence, theology as "scientia" is required if the faith is to be a cogent and credible truth claim.[7]

The cultural middle is made up of people most exposed to competing worldviews because of their location in positions of business and professional leadership. Those on the cultural right can sustain themselves with folk theology because of the local enclaves in which they live. Meanwhile, those on the cultural left with their relativism and individualistic expression can deal with truth as "truth for me" and can, if they so choose, avoid the pressures of disciplined, methodical, systemic thought. For them, journey theology is a more viable offering. But those in the cultural middle are exposed by the very fact that they make decisions and others look to them for the rationales of these decisions. This means that a believable theology will be one that can sustain itself in the face of other views. As a result a theology for the cultural middle will be a variation on theology as sure knowledge. In order to give it less of an academic tone and bring it closer to the lifestyles of business and professional people, I call it explanatory theology.

Explanatory theology grows, in part, out of the occupational experience of cultural-middle people. In business and professional work one of the basic characteristics is the need to explain things. After the diagnosis the physician explains to the patient what is going on and why a particular treatment will be helpful or what treatment options are. An attorney continually explains the law, legal procedure, the best defense, or one legal action as more advantageous than another. A business executive with his or her own staff will provide rationale for company policy or a new sales campaign. In working with customers and other businesses, one must be able to give an accounting for a product, for its quality and price. I recently experienced this myself. During the 1987–1988 school year I was the acting academic dean at Saint Paul School of Theology. In the classroom I had done a lot of explaining; however, I was not prepared for the way I would be consumed by it in that temporary position. Most of my office hours were spent *explaining* a school policy, a faculty action, the student handbook, and on and on. One does not go to church and approach an understanding of the faith without being profoundly influenced by such engrossing occupational experience.

Explanatory theology will also have appeal for people with higher education. Their socialization and training in universities and colleges will lead them to be open to such an approach and prepare them to use it. Hence, Bible study that makes use of critical methods of inquiry will be appreciated, as will opportunities to move into the thought of a contemporary theologian or ethicist. Study of the faith will be an important expression of church programming among cultural-middle people.

Explanatory theology will, then, be most appropriate as one dimension of the approach to meaning in the cultural middle. Being able to relate the faith to other disciplines will be important, and providing alternative ways of looking at personal and social questions is typically appreciated by such people. Again, such explanatory theology will encounter heavy resistance if it makes claims as *the* position or if one attempts to impose a view on the pluralistic, civic orientation of business and professional persons.

In its most powerful form explanatory theology is "thickly descriptive"—to borrow an image from Clifford Geertz but not to use it the same way—meaning that it accounts for human experience and meaning, for the human condition and human liberation, for human deprivation and transformation in a bracing and compelling depiction of the grandeur and the misery of life.[8] At its best, explanatory theology is not an exercise in "musts," "oughts," and "shoulds" but rather a convincing definition or redefinition of the world and our place in it in the presence of God. When explanatory theology is thickly descriptive of the divine-human venture, no exhortation is necessary. Lindsey Pherigo, my colleague in New Testament, once said that good preaching is similar to announcing to a group of people that the building is on fire. One then points out where the fire escape is. He observed that if one adequately describes the situation and gives clear directions to the fire escape, there is no need to tell people what they "ought" to do. So it is with explanatory theology.

One of the criticisms of mainline churches made by a large number of writers and thinkers within the church is that they do not have clear identities. This lack of clarity leaves them without a sharp sense of mission and purpose and without the image necessary to draw people to their membership. It is crucial that the identity of mainline churches be formed theologically. In fact, Roozen, McKinney, and Carroll found that activist churches in Hartford were "grounded in a theology that makes commitment to social justice an explicit and central priority."[9] An explanatory theology that can counter the individualistic, privatistic, controversy-avoidance of cultural-middle lifestyles will be one that offers a more comprehensive account of personal and social issues and one that sets before the churches a vision more compelling than protection of privilege and shifts the ground on which the cross-pressures of business and professional life are usually adjudicated.

Personal Pain and Explanatory Theology

Rock-hard loneliness and the struggle for dignity are at the very center of middle-class pain. The individual competitiveness that leaves one finally alone and the works righteousness that self-deceptively chases worth through achievement condemn middle-class people to a hurried rat race spotted with life crises and the persistent threat of failure. What is needed is a constructive alienation from the ideology of individualism and winning that opens one to a new identity in personal worth and community, understood in a descriptively rich explanatory theology and experienced in empowering group life with others.

It is not enough to tell cultural-middle people that they are accepted. Too often they have heard the simplisms of a preacher or teacher that do not move into the texture of their lives and name the demons. The task of explanatory theology is to describe the landscape of career life and then to point the gospel at the place where it can be heard afresh. In some cases the descriptive task is to lay bare the disemboweling void one anticipates or experiences in failure when the flimsy hope of success is the sustaining ground of one's life. At other times an explanatory theology can identify the working of negative grace, the heavy pressure of God that makes one "sick and tired of being sick and tired" or that moves a person to a new location because the pushing and pulling of God's grace made the old place uninhabitable. Again, in proclamation of this kind it is not necessary to tell people what they ought to do. It is enough to describe the stink or the desolation or the gutting of life and then to point to the surprise of God's lavish gift of grace. The gospel of grace is the most powerful antidote we have in the face of a competitive, achievement culture.

That God accepts us as we are is the good news; that God is not through with us at this point is the call to discipleship. Here the work of explanatory theology is to depict the devastation of the world and to sketch an alternative vision of what God calls us to. The gift of grace is not merely the coming of a warm interiority but also entrance into the reign of God. Justification and justice are inextricable. Liberation and salvation are finally one. God's transformation of the world is at work like leaven.

The task of explanatory theology here is to project a vision of God's reign that can capture the imagination of cultural-middle people because it is more compelling than any vision they know and because it speaks so deeply to the unmet hungers of their own lives. In this connection, I think especially of Jürgen Moltmann's statement of what liberation involves. In economics it is a liberation of substantive justice that guarantees the basic necessities of food, shelter, health, and clothing and the opportunity of people to share duly in the products of their hands. It calls us to a radical redistribution of economic power. Politically, it is the end of oppression, the joining of human dignity and political responsibility, including the rights of all persons to participate in the economic and political decisions so glacially affecting their lives. In cultural terms, liberation is the emancipation of people from alienation and the gain of self-respect and self-confidence through an identity that is recognized and valued by others in community. Moreover, liberation means release from the structural and cyclical pollution of the environment. It is "peace with nature" and movement from a desire to possess nature "to the joy of existing in it." Finally, liberation concerns the meaning of life in the relationship of humanity, society, and nature. It is deliverance from the interior poisoning of life to a living that is significant and "filled with the sense of the whole." The loss of meaning and the condition of godforsakenness are overcome. The conviction of God's indwelling in the world moves in a tidal awakening: "The knowledge of the hidden presence of God in the godforsaken Christ on the cross already gives courage to be, despite nothingness and all annihilating experiences."[10]

Some such vision as that outlined by Moltmann is the task of explanatory theology. Yet it is a task not to be done only by individuals but also in community. The group life of the church can provide the structure for intense sharing, study, and prayer. In the support of such groups the dominant ideologies of individualism and winning can be forcefully critiqued through a caring search for the sources of personal pain. Persons can voice thoughts not often permitted in professional and managerial settings. Moreover, the strength of the group can give people the capacity to take risks, to launch out in new directions, to engage in social action in ways unthinkable in the past. In the next chapter I will report on the work of some churches in moving upper-middle-class people beyond civility and into action.

In sum, the beginning of an approach to cultural-middle business and professional people is by attending to their personal pain and then examining the systemic sources and dimensions of such pain. Moreover, while journey and folk theology speak in a faith idiom appropriate to the cultural left and right respectively, the cultural middle requires yet another approach, that of a thickly descriptive explanatory theology. Such theology will attempt to depict the personal and social dimensions of business and professional life in a more encompassing vision of Christian faith, one committed to redemption, liberation, and transformation.

As we have seen, the cultural middle is quite different from the other two broad cultural lifestyles, as, indeed, each of them is from the others. This obviously poses the question of how mainline churches can include such diversity in congregational life. We will turn to this question in the next chapter.

►Part Five◄

Lifestyles,
Church,
and Christ

▶11◀

The Church and Diverse Lifestyles

How can the church deal respectfully, authentically, and transformatively with the three quite different lifestyles that now characterize U.S. society? In sharpening the differences between the cultural left, middle, and right, I have proposed a sharp challenge for the church, its clergy and laity. Yet it is a challenge that can be met. I believe not only that the church can respond to this challenge but that it will be deeply enhanced by such diversity. Moreover, doing so could lead to a quantum leap in the way the church understands the faith, reckons with and makes moral decisions, celebrates Christian faith, and moves in mission to the world.

Specialization

Perhaps the easiest approach is for a local church to specialize in its ministry to one of the lifestyle groups. Some churches are located in areas or neighborhoods made up predominantly of persons in one of these lifestyles. In such cases a church can appropriately see its mission as that of specialization. Where this is so, however, a church will need to give special attention to its own identity, the image it projects into the community, the style of its pastor, the shape of its program, the format and experience of worship, and so on. In a cultural-right neighborhood church, for example, a major issue may be in dealing with a pastor "on his or her way up" who is unwilling or unable to do ministry authentic to the church members and the people of the neighborhood. Some attempts at transformation are thinly veiled attempts to turn such local churches into upper-middle-class institutions, a deadly exercise in imposition.

To specialize means that a church does need to know who it is and who the people in the community are. My experience in working with laity and clergy in several hundred settings around the country is that they *know* who the church and community are almost as soon as one lays out these lifestyle characteristics and differences. Nevertheless, any church does need to do its demographic homework to make sure that a specialization is in keeping with the congregation and its setting.

In some cases a church begins a specialized ministry to a lifestyle group quite different from its own. In Pittsburg, Kansas, the First United Methodist Church, a cultural-middle congregation, received a large inheritance from a gas well. Not content simply to invest the money, they wanted a ministry in Pittsburg among cultural-right poor people. So they committed $40,000 to this effort. Their senior pastor, Gary Schrag, knew that such a ministry would take more time than he could give it and would require someone whose style was different from his own. The bishop appointed the Rev. Charles F. "Chuck" Kallaus, a lay pastor who has a crew cut and two beautiful tattoos on his forearms. He and his spouse, Caryl, combine both a warm evangelical heart and a burning social compassion. Chuck's instructions were to relate to the people of Pittsburg who lived in a certain area. He was to make himself available in bars, cafés, barbershops, beauty shops—anywhere the people were. As a consultant to the venture I had cautioned First Church about having expectations of success that were too high. I indicated that it would take several years to develop a ministry and a worshiping congregation. Yet within several weeks they had a Sunday school going and in a few months a worshiping congregation. They outgrew the first storefront, rented a second, and by the end of five years had built a new building for their new church. (So much for "experts"!)

The point here is that Chuck and Caryl, cultural-right people themselves, knew how to relate, understood what a church was supposed to be, and were vibrantly effective in their community.

A different kind of example comes from the Reorganized Church of the Latter Day Saints. Wade Hankins realized that his denomination, which had its roots and still many members in the cultural right, was becoming increasingly cultural middle but was not sustaining the participation of baby boomers, especially those on the cultural left. He began what he called Contemporary Christian Centers. Typically, these met in storefronts or other rental property and were aimed quite intentionally at cultural-left baby boomers in theology, worship, music program, and style. This approach immediately spread across the country. At last count they had twenty-five of these centers and were meeting nationally once a year. It remains an effective model of specialization.

Pluralistic Churches

A great many churches will find themselves to be pluralistic in both constituency and community setting. Most mainline churches with more than 200 members will quite likely be congregations of Respectables and Successfuls and will be in some pain about the fact that they are not reaching people under forty-five years of age. While they could specialize principally with one group, that would not typically be an adequate response to the community. So the question becomes one of a church's being able to bear in its congregational life the diversities represented in U.S. culture.

Perhaps the first thing to be said is something that is already true of many local churches: A church effective in reaching diverse lifestyles will be a congregation of congregations. Each subcongregation then specializes in worship, caring, programming, and outreach that are congruent with a particular lifestyle. I am suggesting that this be quite intentional. It is my contention in this regard that a lot of churches presently composed of Respectables and Successfuls would be much better served if the church were more sharply differentiated in worship and program. Many Respectables deny themselves, for example, by continuing to be a part of worship services aimed at the upper middle class. The sermons are framed in language and style to address the college-educated, not to deal with the intensely local questions and tight kinship circles of the cultural right. In other settings the Successful and the Conflicted may be part of a dominantly Respectable congregation and feel unaddressed by the interests and style of most of those in the congregation. These problems deepen when one seeks to reach the cultural left, Strivers, the Hard Living, and the Desperately Poor.

How can specialization within a congregation be addressed? In some churches alternative worship services are feasible and needed. It is not unthinkable at all that one service could be basically cultural right in substance and in style and another cultural middle. I have already suggested worship opportunities for baby boomers at times other than Sunday morning.

In most churches, however, it will not be possible to have that many specialized worship services. Such settings require liturgy and preaching that are alert to congregational differences and that can have "something for everyone." For example, if the sermon addresses a moral question such as abortion, it will be important to examine the issue in terms of the family and local relations of the cultural right, from a pragmatic and informed explanatory sense for managers and professionals, and in terms of self-fulfillment, concern about relationship, and social consciousness on the cultural left. These concerns can be expressed in a theological framework that gives them meaning and power for diverse lifestyles. Clearly, one cannot go through such a maze of values in every sermon, but an artful weaving of these in the preaching task and a sensitive indication to lifestyle groups that one understands and cares is certainly within the competence of mainline clergy.

Of major assistance in preaching at this point is the use of stories, which have an amazing capacity to communicate across lifestyle differences. Whether these be biblical narratives or stories drawn from contemporary life, they have a powerful attraction for the broad diversity of U.S. people.[1] In liturgy there is also room to touch the interests and concerns of diverse lifestyles and to place them in the context of worship and the adoration of God.

Yet the brunt of the diversity of mainline churches will have to be carried in church programming, primarily in the church school and a wide range of small-group activities. The use of multiple choirs and a variety of study groups, prayer circles, devotional meetings, community service, and social action projects seem to be the best way to provide participation that is both intrinsically honest for the people involved and representative of their style.

Staffing

Adequate staffing is necessary for a congregation of congregations, and two criteria about church programming that come from Lyle Schaller are quite relevant here.

First, as we have seen, Schaller suggests that a church needs five or six fellowship groups for every hundred members. His point is that small groups provide the basic means for assimilating and sustaining the participation of people in the lifestyle of the church. My point, in addition, would be that a group life of this numerical strength could also provide a plethora of options shaped and aimed at diverse lifestyles.[2]

Second, Schaller maintains that a church needs the equivalent of one full-time program staff person for every hundred attenders on an average Sunday morning. These are *program* staff. As important as secretaries and custodians are, if they do not do programming, they do not count in this formula. These program staff people can be full-time or part-time and they can be paid or volunteer. What is important is that there be enough staff to provide support for the group life of the church.[3]

I would also suggest that staff be selected in terms of lifestyle representativeness. The presence, for example, of a Chuck Kallaus on a church staff would do much to guarantee the presence of a strong cultural-right contingency. His evangelical and social justice interests would be of genuine value in shaping programs in a transformative direction. In addition, the presence of a baby boomer with a keen sensitivity for the cultural left would make all the difference in reaching out to young adults in the area. Meanwhile, the senior pastor or some other staff person may possess the gifts and graces to reach professionals and business managers. I think especially of the work Lamar Davis did in Rogers, Arkansas, as an associate pastor with a large group of cultural-middle people. His theological expertise and administrative skills, on the one hand, and his ability to draw part-time, volunteer, and paid staff into the program, on the other, brought together a highly motivated group of business and professional people in a rich group-life approach to community and discipleship.

Programming

Different styles and formats will be necessary and appropriate for working in a lifestyle-diverse congregation of congregations. What follows is perhaps overly distinctive for each lifestyle group in the church, but it is heuristic in order to provide illustrative handles for thinking through, planning, and carrying out programs.

With respect to cultural-left baby boomers and Strivers a detailed programmatic response to them was suggested in chapter 3. At this point a summary will suffice in order to juxtapose this approach to those of the cultural middle and right. Cultural-left programming will be framed in a journey theology that appreciates the autobiographical and developmental process of participants. It will find legitimate, theologically informed ways to deal with the therapeutic-mystical interests of baby boomers. Moreover, the cultural left is the most sensitive to social issues and the most liberal in the political spectrum. Large numbers of them will appreciate efforts to address ecological, social justice, and peace issues. They will respond especially to concrete, hands-on opportunities to be involved in missional outreach endeavors. Programs for singles and for couples with children will be welcomed, as will a vital music program. These all need to be structured so as to be sensitive to very busy people, the structure of whose lives may not articulate with the usual church schedule.

Programs for the cultural right will be quite different. Most of these people will be more denominationally identified and will appreciate some attention to the history and beliefs of their church, provided it is not too academic and "stuffy." Some will want a strong "orthodox" orientation and definite creedal understandings of the faith. Fundamentalists will tend to be quite interested here. Evangelicals will focus more on conversion, and the pentecostals and charismatics will focus on experience. Nevertheless, a church can provide for these differences, if the church's identity is one where such differences are welcomed and appreciated. The folk theology of the cultural right will take scripture quite seriously, and they will appreciate church school classes, Bible study, and prayer circles that make the Bible central to their work. Authentic moral reasoning for them will take folk theology, traditional values, and conventional morality seriously. This means that when an issue is addressed, thoughtful and respectful attention needs to be given to the local and family relationships and the impact of decisions on them. A sensitive reading of their view of the world and a responsive dealing with the difficulties of cultural-right people will open a much wider attention on their part to emerging social and ethical issues. It will provide an opportunity to see these in terms of the lived reality of their own lives. For the most part these are politically moderate people who can be approached on contemporary questions quite directly when the approach is sensitive to and coheres with their approach to meaning. Their socio-moral conservatism is an especially powerful basis for commitment. There is no reason why this cannot take liberative and transformative direction, provided that church leaders work within the realities of their world and their frame of discourse.

People on the cultural right will enjoy service projects and will especially appreciate opportunities to help people in need, which is not only an occasion for compassion but can also be a learning experience for examining the deeper systemic issues that typically underlie human need. Local people enjoy gatherings: church suppers, festive occasions, homecomings, church school socials, picnics, church property cleanups, Christmas pageants, and so on. In short, a traditional church program speaks to them and provides an opportunity for new direction.

Let me be clear here: It is not my intention to *use* cultural-right people to struggle for someone else's issues. I am concerned about the church responding at a deeper level to *their* interests. The women and men who hold fast to popular religion have good reasons for seeing the world as an evil place and for feeling powerless before it. These systemic demons, these principalities and powers, need to be named in the language of the cultural right so that a social exorcism can begin. If such matters are addressed, the cultural right will make a significant contribution to the struggles of other people in the United States and elsewhere. Moreover, I am not trying to suggest ways that clergy can get cultural-right people to take on the former's agenda. It is more important that the clergy learn to address the interests and liberative needs of local people. The more important question in this context is, How do global issues of the economy, political decision-making, and the like strike local people, and how can they be addressed theologically, ethically, politically, and organizationally in terms of the understanding and lived experience of the cultural right?

As for programming with the cultural middle, mainline churches are better equipped and stylized to reach them than any other class or lifestyle group, with the possible exception of Respectables. The interests of the clergy, the organizational format of the church, the increased rationalization of decision-making, and so on fit with the occupational experience of the cultural middle and give continuity to their experience. What needs more attention than anything else in programming is to upgrade the quality. Cultural-middle people will have high expectations of their church in terms of professional staff, informative church school classes that provide a significant experience of community, the opportunity to participate and lead in a well-managed church, and the discovery of a deepening spiritual life. Quality preaching, teaching, community life, and service draw business and professional people especially.

It may be that the biggest challenge facing the church is the cultural middle, because they are the most central leaders of the church and of the community. Their location in the highly privileged sector of U.S. life and its powerfully constraining boundaries, on the one hand, and their individualism, activism, privatism, conservatism, and civility, on the other, make them the most difficult to reach and move in a liberative and transformative direction. In all likelihood the kind of change I would like to see will not come from them, although some will provide leadership for it. More basic changes will come from pressures within and beyond the United States. So, as I have suggested, the most realistic approach is one that addresses business managers and professionals at the point of their own pain: the stress, the striving for dignity through success, the failure, the life crises, and the pressures on family life. These issues and others require a deeply descriptive handling by the power of explanatory theology. It is perhaps at this point that a new and deeper commitment to liberation and change is possible. A more profound understanding of God and the world and the systemic dimension of personal and existential struggle can be appropriated here. Yet theology alone is not adequate without its being embodied in community. This needs to be considered in relationship to the matter of civility.

Civility

Let me confess the strangeness I feel in "opposing" civility. One never appreciates civility sufficiently until social life is without it. Let it be clear that I oppose totalitarian programs in a society or a church, even when they are subtle, and I have no truck with the imposition of one group's will on another that disregards due governance process and the rightful claims of opponents. Rather, the concern here is with an etiquette that has developed within mainline churches and that operates to mitigate commitment and paralyze action.

In a church composed of diverse lifestyles this etiquette of civility is likely to be even stronger. How can commitment and action be vouchsafed without violating the rights of others who hold different views? Lyle Schaller has suggested a policy that amounts to counting the *yes* votes, meaning that the church will have a number of programs in which the governing board neither approves nor disapproves a particular effort or action. Instead, those who are interested are free to support and participate in the effort. It is understood that those who participate do so as a group and do not implicate others in the church, either by speaking or acting for them.[4]

A procedure similar to this has been used by the First Christian Church of St. Joseph, Missouri, where Charles H. Bayer as pastor has worked to carry out the implications of liberation theology in an affluent middle-class congregation. After building the case theologically for political involvement, he suggests that churches need small groups or units of risk takers, which he sees operating much like base communities. Such a group in his congregation, the Shalom Task Force, organized a petition drive on the nuclear freeze and, working with similar groups in the city, was able to get a unanimous positive vote from the city council on the resolution. They brought several thousand signatures on a petition, and a chamber full of people pressed for its adoption. Such small groups, networked with others, can be very effective. The minority of people of the cultural middle who are prepared to take such risks can find significant avenues for action.[5] Such base communities do not need approval from a church board, provided that they are acting on their own.

Bayer has worked to make sure that such groups are prepared and well informed. He has taken study very seriously in developing these small-group social action units and has organized two extended courses of study, one on the Bible and the other on liberation theology. In the Bible study, students not only develop a grounding in the biblical materials but see them from the perspective of the liberating work of God. In the study of liberation theology, Bayer has written and published *A Guide to Liberation Theology for Middle Class Congregations*. These courses of study are demanding. The Bible study is two years in length and requires note taking, assignments, and prompt attendance. If a class is missed, the student is asked to listen to the tape of the lecture and discussion. Bayer reports that two thirds of the students complete the course.[6]

Bayer maintains, also, that study and action are to be simultaneous, not separate activities, and he reports a number of ways in which this is done by congregations around the United States, such as sanctuary movements, a celebration of the Fourth of July focused on liberation, the use of stockholdings in pressuring corporations away from repressive policies, member visits to Third World countries, letter writing and confrontational visits with legislators, and the deepening of liturgy. worship, and preaching on the issues of oppression and liberation.[7]

Finally, Bayer deals with deeply personal issues, which he sees as having systemic roots. Middle-class people are caught, he attests, in boredom, alcohol, and drug abuse and what he calls "the prophylactic personality," the person who lives "without risk, without adventure. It is the well-protected, safe, orderly, careful life. Boundaries are set."[8] Bayer believes that new life can be offered to such middle-class people through a mission that involves risk and action and the support of small groups on the base community model.

I appreciate very much Bayer's work and his witness. I would also want to affirm the need to address the concerns of the cultural right as I have detailed them. His model, though, has rich potential for working with the cultural middle and the cultural left and for finding a way past the paralyzing etiquette of civility.

Clergy and Theological Education

The lifestyle diversity of the United States places heavy demands on clergy. There is a real need for clergy to become "trilingual" and "tripraxis," meaning by that to develop a capacity to communicate and to reflect and act in ways conversant with each of the broad lifestyles suggested here. Such competence would deeply enrich the lives of many congregations, which could then sense that their pastor deeply understood them. When he or she dealt with liberation and social justice issues, they would feel that they too were authentically a part of that concern. So many people in the church today feel left out in worship and preaching and program because *they* are not addressed. This is especially so in sermons about the social witness of the church. Clergy more sensitive and able to make the connection between the personal struggles of the congregation and the social injustices of the world would be an inspiring channel of grace, offering that special pastoral care that comes when people feel they have been *met* and *known*.

In working with the cultural left, clergy will find it necessary to work outside traditional church patterns; while working with the cultural right, they will need to move to a new appreciation for traditional expressions and local people. The cultural middle poses the challenge of a ministry critical of what is most highly valued in the culture while remaining alert and compassionate to their personal pain. Lifestyle-specific ministry is a demanding job but one replete with possibilities. Moreover, it opens up new avenues for ministry and new ways to define old problems and conflicts, which have often festered for lack of explicit attention to specific lifestyles, concerns, and issues. Lifestyle-specific ministry provides new approaches, new tools, and new understandings to move into areas not fully identified or appreciated in most church settings. It is a gift, if you will, for the late twentieth century with which the church can reach new people and speak with greater discernment.

Lifestyle-specific ministry also holds many implications for theological education. The discipline of theology itself with its social location among professionalism in universities and theological schools has a major task in understanding and stating the faith in ways that respect the approaches to meaning diversely operating among people in the church and the world. Liberation theology—Third World, feminist, black—has perhaps made the major contribution to theology in the latter part of this century, and it has major implications for local theologies of the cultural left, middle, and right.

Theological education will need to come to a new appreciation for the cultural right. Except for the poor, such folk receive little attention in theological schools in the United States, and theology remains too confined to Schreiter's scientia type, largely academic and not adequately developed in forms that are authentic to other communities. It would be extremely valuable if, for example, scripture were studied in terms of approaches that spoke to different lifestyles. Or church administration, which has been too much "kept" by contemporary management theory and practice as developed in corporate America, could have an explosion in theory and praxis if it attempted to develop communal approaches fitted for the cultural right and alternative approaches for the inner-directed self-fulfillment lifestyles of the cultural left. I am personally excited about what it will mean to do Christian ethics in a cultural-right framework, one that is responsive to the local and global, evangelical and social justice imperatives of the Christian faith.

An orientation that takes local theology seriously and develops approaches and models that are context-specific, liberative, and transformative would bring a revolution in theology and in the training of clergy and laity. It would also move toward a closing of the gulf that so often separates the theological schools and the churches. This gulf is a factor in the church's distance from the world, a theological problem in Christian faith of enormous magnitude.

►12◄

The Christ in Culture Transforming Culture

In preceding chapters I have intimated that the theological basis of my concern to develop approaches to ministry indigenous to different lifestyles grows out of a conviction that Christ is already *in* any culture and working to transform it. We can now turn our attention to this theological conviction and spell out what it means in more detail.

Christ and Culture. In his classic work *Christ and Culture*, H. Richard Niebuhr addresses what he calls "the enduring problem" of the relationship of the revelation in Christ to the prevailing patterns of culture.[1] As I have posed the question here, What is the relationship of Christ to the major lifestyle groups suggested in these pages? Do we simply "baptize" lifestyles? Do we reject them altogether? What, indeed, is an appropriate theological response? How does the church respond to the indigenous lifestyles of a people?

In his review of the history of the church, Niebuhr suggests that there are five basic types of relationship between Christ and culture.[2] The first of these is one that emphasizes the opposition of Christ *against* culture. In this view Christ is against the customs and human achievements of any given time and place and poses an either-or decision to the church. Niebuhr cites the First Letter of John, Tertullian, and Tolstoy as examples of this approach to the relation of Christ and culture. Here the responsibility of the church would be to stand in opposition to any lifestyle.

The second type is that of the Christ *of* culture, a view that holds to a basic agreement between Christ and culture where Jesus is regarded as a cultural hero, where his life and teachings represent the very heights of human achievement, and where the values of a culture find their consummate expression in him. Those who tend to equate U.S. culture with Christianity would be contemporary expressions of this view. In the history of the church the Gnostics, Abelard, and A. Ritschl are listed as examples by Niebuhr. In this view the implication is to endorse lifestyles as Christian.

Christ *above* culture is a third type detailed by Niebuhr. Here Christ comes to culture from above, offering values and meaning not otherwise available to human pursuits. In this view Christ is the fulfillment and the completion of culture, hence in this sense a Christ of culture. Yet what Christ offers does not arise from culture but, indeed, must be brought to it from above. So Christ is *of* culture as its completion but *above* culture as the heavenly source of its fulfillment. This synthesis of the continuity and discontinuity of Christ and culture are best represented by Thomas Aquinas. In this view a given lifestyle is completed by God's offering of grace from above.

The fourth type, Christ and culture *in paradox,* maintains that a Christian must live, really, in two worlds: one, a world of ultimate obedience to Christ and the other a world of penultimate obedience to the culture. For a Christian two moralities compete for the support of a Christian, and neither of them can be avoided. Yet they inevitably will be in conflict, and the Christian lives continually in the paradox of this relationship. The apostle Paul and Luther are two examples named by Niebuhr. In terms of lifestyle issues this view would recognize that we are inevitably socialized and hence cultural creatures. To be sure, one may change one's lifestyle, but one will always *have* a lifestyle. The question, then, is one of the relationship of Christ to a pattern of living, the paradoxical relation between being a socially conditioned, historically located creature and, at the same time, responsible to Christ.

The final type is the conversionist approach in which Christ is the *transformer* of culture. According to Niebuhr this view actually combines two views of the relation of Christ to culture. On the one hand, the conversionist view recognizes the opposition between Christ and the institutions and customs of a society, but this does not result in a separation and otherworldliness by Christians or in a sheer endurance that simply awaits salvation beyond history. On the other hand, the conversionist approach sees Christ changing and transforming humanity in culture. In Niebuhr's view there is no nature without culture and no turning away from sin and evil to God except in society. The examples of this view are Augustine and F. D. Maurice. The conversionist view has a clear implication for lifestyle issues. Lifestyles are, first, in opposition to Christ and, second, being transformed by Christ.

The Christ in Culture. From what has gone before, it should be clear that my point of view falls clearly in the Christ-transforming-culture camp, but I do have a qualification of the position as described by Niebuhr. I am troubled that Niebuhr combines only the Christ against culture and the Christ-transforming culture in the conversionist view. This leaves no affirmation of lifestyles by Christian faith. If Christ only opposes and transforms, I wonder what God's acceptance of us can finally mean in acts of justifying grace. If lifestyle can be only opposed and transformed, what can really be accepted? Human beings are not ciphers devoid of social content; we are cultural beings. To be accepted by God is to be accepted, in part, *as* cultural beings; otherwise we are not finally accepted. By limiting the conversionist approach to Christ's opposing and transforming culture, Niebuhr makes this view an abstract purism. It may preserve the integrity of the Christian witness, but it absents itself of concrete, living, culturally located human beings.

I believe instead that the Christ-transforming-culture view is best combined with a Christ-*in*-culture view rather than a Christ-*against*-culture view only. A Christ-in-culture view provides the opportunity for both critique and affirmation. To take a Christ-against-culture view as the initial moment in the conversionist approach, strictly understood, denies in fact the transforming action of Christ in the past that would be existent now—even though in partial and broken ways—in *any* present. That is, if Christ can only oppose a lifestyle in the conversionist view, this implies that Christ has not been transforming such lifestyles in the past.

So my view is one of the Christ in culture transforming culture. Let it be clear that the task of critique is a basic dimension of this view. It is also important to affirm the transforming action of God cumulatively present in cultural formations of the here and now, the Christ concretely present in the lives of real people.

Such a view, it seems to me, is deeply biblical. In the space available here I want to demonstrate the relationship of a Christ-in-culture-transforming-culture view to the Gospel of John. As much as any book in the New Testament, John has rich implications for this point of view.[3]

The Gospel of John and the Christ in Culture. John's Gospel begins with a Christological view of creation. "In the beginning was the Word . . . all things were made through [the Word]," the *Logos* of God (John 1:1,3). The Christ in culture, in history, in nature, in the *kosmos* (world) is the Christ in whom and through whom all things were made. In its created source the world is not alien to Christ but rather is brought into being and framed by the Word.

This is not a naïve assertion in John because the Fourth Gospel understands the power of evil in the world. The Gospel is filled with depictions of the perversity of the kosmos. While the world is one made in and through the Word, it is also a world now twisted into bondage, illusion, and death. The world is a place organized around all the wrong values and is a world opposed to God. Perhaps no place in the Fourth Gospel reveals this perversity more sharply than the tumultuous conflict of chapter 8. There the religious leaders of Jesus' time claim a freedom from illusion and bondage that only confirms their mendacity and captivity. The chapter ends as they in their fury take up stones to throw at Jesus, a foreshadowing of the later conspiracy to kill him.

Even so, as perverse as the world is, it is not only a kosmos made in and through Christ, but one in which "the Word became flesh and dwelt among us" (1:14). The word for "dwell" here is *skēnoō* in the Greek and has the literal meaning that God pitched tent with us. This word primarily conveys the intimate relationship God has with us, although some commentators suggest that *skēnoō* means that the presence of Christ will be temporary: that is, Jesus' ministry will be but for a short time. Nevertheless, the dwelling of God is with us because God so loved the kosmos and gave Christ that we may have eternal life.

Eternal life offers the world life of a new kind. Rather than *psuche* (our natural life without God), Christ brings *aionios zōē* (eternal life). This is life as only God has it—as the world in its perversity cannot have it or know it. In John's Gospel *zōē* has a radically contemporaneous character. Eternal life is not simply put off beyond history but, in Christ, is powerfully present in the here and now so that the crucial matter is that one *have* life in the present.

As such, *zōē* not only transforms but completes life. In place of the bondage of the kosmos, *zōē* brings freedom against the lies and illusions of the world, offers the truth of Christ, and in the face of death is life eternal. As evidence of this transformative life John offers signs as Jesus changes water into wine, heals the sick and afflicted, feeds the multitude, raises Lazarus, and walks on water to meet the disciples. Furthermore, Jesus is the bread of heaven, living water, the light of the world, the bearer of the truth, preexistent before Abraham, the resurrection and the life, and one with God.

There is perhaps no more clearly transformative chapter in John's Gospel than the thirteenth. This is the last supper with the disciples. In the synoptics it is the time of Jesus' sharing of bread and wine as his body and blood in remembrance of him and in anticipation of his coming again. Yet in John's Gospel there is no eucharist, no words of institution. In fact, the only dipping of a morsel of any kind is that of Judas, who does it on the way out the door to betray Jesus. At this very point John reports that Satan entered Judas (13:27).

Why this enormous gap in the tradition? John certainly must have known about the supper. He wrote sometime after 85 c.e., and the Lord's Supper was well established by this time. Certainly its absence in the thirteenth chapter is not because the Lord's Supper is unimportant to John (see John 6:53–59). Moreover, it is not for a lack of a sacramental view of life in John. Indeed, as Christ is the Word through which the world was created and as John continually in the gospel relates Christ to the most concrete things in the creation—air, water, light, bread, and so on—he is profoundly sacramental. No adequate reason offers itself except perhaps the one some scholars suggest: To wit, by the time of John's writing the church has a history of some fifty or sixty years. By then abuses of the Lord's Supper have begun, inequalities are growing in the church, and competition for status and leadership is marring the community of faith. In this thirteenth chapter is a stunning critique of such ambition and bickering.

It is not accidental, then, that in place of the eucharist John focuses on the washing of the disciples' feet by Jesus. In those days only two sorts of people washed feet, women and slaves. The point must not be missed that this is the Logos made flesh who has identified himself with slaves and women. The Word made flesh now appears with those who are at the very bottom of society, and this solidarity and this work become the model of discipleship. Along with this act comes a new commandment that we love one another even as Christ loved us.

This event with its graphic portrayal of Judas dipping the morsel and of Christ washing feet could hardly be more stark in contrast; the traitor who consumes the "Lord's Supper" and has Satan enter him and the Word becoming woman and slave. The values and patterns of the society are radically called into question and turned upside down.

Even so, it is not a Christ separated from the world but enfleshed in it. It is not a Christ who stands outside the culture of his time, but who is deeply involved in it. For example, Jesus identifies with the common and lowliest people of his time. He observes a courteous ritual of hospitality like foot washing and reinterprets its meaning. He makes preparation to observe the Passover, giving it new purpose and a new commandment. These are examples of the Christ of culture.

In the thirteenth chapter, Christ is the Christ *in* culture. One finds there affirmation of traditional patterns of his own culture and a startling identification with slaves and women. Yet there is also a searing judgment of betrayal and a pointed critique of the church in the time of John. These are followed by a new transformative commandment and a call to become a community identifiable by its love (13:34–35). This is the Christ affirming, opposing, and transforming culture.

One point, for our purposes, needs yet to be made. In his crucifixion Christ is "lifted up" according to John and glorified. And then on that reality-altering Sunday morning he is resurrected, making his first appearances in John to the women. Jesus in the Fourth Gospel, both before the crucifixion and after, tells the confused disciples that he must go away but that he will not leave them without a Comforter. The promise of the coming of the Spirit is made over and over again in the Gospel.

The point here is that the *skēnē*, the pitched tent, the temporary dwelling of Jesus with the disciples will end, and soon, but in his place the Spirit will come. Here it is utterly crucial to understand that the Spirit will take on the functions of Christ. Not only will the Spirit be with the disciples, but the Spirit now becomes the ongoing source of divine *zōē*-giving vitality. The Spirit now becomes the power of life and truth and freedom moving and working in the kosmos to counter its falsehood, bondage, and death.

This is the Spirit that blows where it will, that is not subject to the constraints of the natural order, the human community, or the vicissitudes of history. The Spirit is *loose* in the world, and the Word of God through which and by which the kosmos was created is now moving in the world to transform the world.

This is profoundly good news. The Spirit of Christ precedes us into the world. This Spirit is already at work in any society, any culture, any lifestyle, and absolutely nothing can stop this redemptive, liberative, and transformative power. The task of the church, then, is to seek out the Spirit of Christ, to discern the current of saving work, to affirm—wherever it appears—authentic, qualitative life *(zōē)* and to call into question the bondage, illusion, and death of a twisted world. This means that we are not called to go anywhere where Christ has not already gone ahead to open the way, so that we are able to go confident in the moving power of the Spirit. This is a bracing framework in which to pursue ministry among the lifestyles of any culture, including our own.

The Christ in culture is the Christ transforming culture. This is the source of our hope for the immediate future and finally for the completion of the creation and the reign of God. Our task is to see Christ in the faces of those where we do not expect to do so and to be hospitable to the messianic work afoot. To love Christ, and to love the neighbor in whom Christ comes, is to respect the journey over which the neighbor has come, to appreciate the struggles to make and keep life together, and not to miss the failure or the pain of those who seem to have it made. In the midst of all of these, we can trust that the Spirit of Christ is there and that the work of transformation is already under way.

This affirmation has come to take on a deeply personal and existential meaning for me. Our son Steven was killed in February of 1988 when a man, unable to see because of the glare of the sun, stopped twice at the stop sign, but then entered the intersection and hit Steve on his motorcycle. Steve was probably brain dead a few minutes after the collision, but his strong constitution and great heart fought around the clock. The last six hours his heart raced at 160 beats per minute, working furiously to hold up his dropping blood pressure. When it could no longer sustain the pace, his heart slowed to less than half that rate, and the loss of blood pressure brought an end to his unconscious but valiant effort.

Steve had been an alcoholic and an abuser of other drugs for ten or twelve years. During that long agonizing time we gave up five or six times a year, believing that his situation was hopeless, that not even God could answer our seemingly endless prayers. He seemed beyond help and even beyond the teachings of Al-Anon and "tough love." Through those years we saw him in so many painful and devastating conditions, injured after car wrecks, motorcycle accidents, and even one severe electroshock that very nearly killed him; we visited him in jails, in hospitals, in drug rehab programs, in a seemingly endless series of cheap apartments; we watched him lose one job after another, break up with at least a dozen women, and dissolve one marriage; we winced at broken noses, lacerations, bruises, and black eyes from fights; we witnessed his "decision" to go on the wagon time and again, and we spent those treadmill nights unable to sleep and gutted by worry and fear. It seemed that nothing worked and nothing seemed to be going on in his life that could pull him out of his drug dependency. I felt he was God forsaken.

Eight months before his death he entered an inner-city drug abuse center and went cold turkey because he was "sick and tired of being sick and tired" and because his fiancée, Nancy, had already preceded him there by some six weeks. From that point on, he never used alcohol or any other drug again. During the last months we enjoyed a relationship with him we had dreamed of ever since he was fourteen, when his first troubles began. He, his brother, and I built a solar room on the house that is now named after him; he won a trophy in the Kansas City Motorcycle Show and delighted in taking us around to explain what had been done to different bikes. He and Nancy went home to Mississippi with us at Thanksgiving to see his grandparents, and, sober, he celebrated Christmas with us, buying everyone presents that "aren't practical," but that "y'all would enjoy." He began working at the Kansas City Community Center, which he had entered earlier. Active in AA, he met with many groups and soon became the person they called to work with those just released from prison. He began speaking around the city and joined Visions, an AA motorcycle club, and discovered a new set of friends and a vital purpose in his life. Through them he finally found his "church." He got a job in a chemical company and was working steadily. Two weeks before he died he was offered a new job that paid considerably more and would have enabled him and Nancy to be married.

On the day he was killed—a sun-filled, uncharacteristically warm day in February—his award-winning bike had too much paint on an electrical circuit, interrupting the work of the generator and depleting the battery. The bike stopped right in front of a body shop on Highway 116 near Lathrop, Missouri. Expecting rejection because he and his friends were on motorcycles, when they went into the body shop they discovered that the owner was a deputy sheriff, making Steve quite apprehensive. Steve asked Roger and Tammy, friends on the other bike, if they would talk to the shop owner. Even though dried out, Steve was still not comfortable with law enforcement officials. But when they approached the man, he could not have been nicer or more helpful. They fixed the connection and recharged the battery. He told them of his own son's love of motorcycles and how much he enjoyed working with his son on them. Also, he mentioned that his son had been injured in a military-service-related accident and that he was waiting to get a flight to go see him. Steve was touched by the man's help and his sharing with them.

Nancy, who was not seriously hurt in the accident, told us later that, as they were about to leave, Steve stopped and quietly looked at the body shop and the man standing some distance away.

"You see," she said, "Steve had been having some experiences that he simply could no longer deny. He felt that a supreme Being was working in his life. He couldn't believe how so many things were working out for him. He just knew there was something beyond him, a power helping him straighten out his life. He just wanted things right and to do things right. And it was working."

After Roger and Tammy got on their bike and Nancy climbed on the back of theirs, she said that Steve looked at them, looked back at the deputy sheriff, and said, "You know, this stuff really works."

Those were the last words anyone ever heard him say. He put on his helmet and drove six miles to the intersection of highways 116 and 33.

Notes

Full publishing information not given here may be found in the bibliography.

Introduction

1. See *Religion in America—50 Years: 1935–1985* (Princeton, N.J.: Gallup Report no. 236, 1985) for religious trends over the past fifty years. Also see Thomas Ferguson and Joel Rogers, "The Myth of America's Turn to the Right," *Atlantic Monthly*, May 1986, 43–53. This article summarized public opinion research demonstrating that no turn to the right has occurred politically in the United States in the last ten years. It also indicates a continuing liberalization of socio-moral issues. There are some exceptions to this generalization, but the trend is clearly sustained.

Chapter 1
Shifting Values: Self-Fulfillment vs. Self-Denial

1. Karen Greenwaldt and Warren J. Hartman, "A Generation Coming of Age," *Discipleship Trends* 3(4):1–4 (Aug. 1985).

2. U.S. Senate Special Committee on Aging in Conjunction with the American Association of Retired Persons, *Aging America: Trends and Projections*, 184. See also Tex Sample, "The Elderly Poor, the Future, and the Church," *Journal of Religion and Aging* 3(1/2):121–140 (fall/winter 1986).

3. Daniel Yankelovich, *New Rules: Searching for Self-Fulfillment in a World Turned Upside Down*, 111–114.

4. See Tex Sample, *Blue Collar Ministry*, 71–84.

5. Yankelovich, *New Rules*, 21.

6. Ibid., 6–13.

7. Ibid., 7.

8. Ibid., 174.

9. Robert Bellah et al., *Habits of the Heart: Individualism and Commitment in American Life*, 33.

10. Yankelovich, *New Rules*, 188–189.

11. With roughly 165 million people eighteen years of age and older in the United States this means that about 28 million people have the strong form. This number differs from that of Arnold Mitchell, who

finds 33 million inner-directed people in the United States. Such differences result from Yankelovich's focus on self-fulfillment and Mitchell's focus on inner direction. It is clear, however, that they are working with the same group of people. Sharper agreement in number would occur if their data banks could be brought together in a conversation with similar definitions of concepts. See Mitchell's *The Nine American Lifestyles*, 112ff.

12. Yankelovich, *New Rules*, 91.

13. Dean R. Hoge and David A. Roozen, eds., *Understanding Church Growth and Decline: 1950–1978*, 327–330.

14. Ibid.

15. Ibid., 199–205.

16. *What Lies Ahead: Looking Toward the '90's* (Alexandria, Va.: United Way of America, 1987), 12.

17. Haviland Houston, speech before the Missouri Area Pastors' School, Fayette, Missouri, Jan. 12, 1988.

18. Yankelovich, *New Rules*, 246.

19. Ibid., 251–253, 257.

Chapter 2
Who Are the Cultural Left?

1. Arnold Mitchell, *The Nine American Lifestyles*, 15–17.

2. Ibid., 15–22.

3. Ibid., 22.

4. Lillie Wilson, "The Aging of Aquarius," *American Demographics*, Sept. 1988, 34.

5. Quoted in Wilson, "Aging of Aquarius," 36.

6. Ibid., 61.

7. Ibid., 60.

8. Ted Peters, "Discerning the Spirits of the New Age," *Christian Century*, Aug. 31–Sept. 7, 1988, 764–765.

9. Carl Dudley, *Where Have All the People Gone?* (New York: Pilgrim Press, 1979), 11–17.

10. Dean R. Hoge and David A. Roozen, eds., *Understanding Church Growth and Decline: 1950–1978*, 327–330.

Chapter 3
Strategy for Reaching the Cultural Left

1. Warren J. Hartman, speech before the National Consultation on Reaching for the Baby Boomers, Sept. 2, 1988.

2. Yoshio Fukuyama distinguished between middle-class religion oriented around "thinking and doing" and working-class religion that

focused on "believing and feeling." See his "The Major Dimensions of Church Membership," *Review of Religious Research* 2(4):154ff. (spring 1961).

3. Lyle Schaller, *Assimilating New Members* (Nashville: Abingdon Press, 1979), 5.

4. Arnold Mitchell, *The Nine American Lifestyles*, 20–22.

5. Martha Farnsworth Riche, speech before the National Consultation on Reaching for the Baby Boomers, Sept. 2, 1988.

6. Quoted in Karen Greenwaldt and Warren J. Hartman, "A Generation Coming of Age," *Discipleship Trends* 3(4):3–4 (Aug. 1985).

7. *What Lies Ahead* (Alexandria, Va.: United Way of America, 1987), 12.

8. Hartman, National Consultation speech.

9. Interview with Karen Greenwaldt, Sept. 2, 1988.

10. See, for example, Lyle Schaller, *Growing Plans* (Nashville: Abingdon Press, 1983), 72f.

11. Riche, National Consultation speech.

Chapter 4
Journey Theology

1. Alvin Toffler, *Future Shock* (New York: Bantam Books, 1971).

2. Martha Farnsworth Riche, speech before the National Consultation on Reaching for the Baby Boomers, Sept. 2, 1988.

3. I am indebted in this section to Robert J. Schreiter, *Constructing Local Theologies;* see his discussion of Theology as Wisdom, 85–87. Schreiter, of course, is not responsible for the way I have interpreted his work.

4. See James Atlas, "Beyond Demographics," *Atlantic Monthly*, Oct. 1984, 51.

5. Schreiter, *Constructing Local Theologies*, 87.

6. This is Walter G. Muelder's phrase. See his *The Ethical Edge of Christian Theology* (New York: Edwin Mellen Press, 1983), 7.

7. See especially Robert Wuthnow, "Recent Patterns of Secularization: A Problem of Generations?" *American Sociological Review* 41:850–867 (Oct. 1976).

8. William Greider, "The Rolling Stone Survey," *Rolling Stone*, April 7, 1988, 34–38.

9. W. Paul Jones, *Theological Worlds* (Nashville: Abingdon Press, 1989).

10. Ted Peters, "Discerning the Spirits of the New Age," *Christian Century*, Aug. 31–Sept. 7, 1988, 765–766.

11. The phrase is James Weldon Johnson's in *God's Trombones* (New York: Viking Press, 1955).

Chapter 5
Who Are the Cultural Right?

1. Paul Tillich, *Systematic Theology*, vol. 3 (Chicago: University of Chicago Press, 1963), 300–426.

2. Robert Merton, *Social Theory and Social Structure*, rev. and enl. (Glencoe, Ill.: Free Press, 1957), 387–420.

3. Emilia E. Martinez-Brawley, "Crisis and Conflict in the Heartland: Social Work's Challenges and Opportunities," keynote address to Iowa NASW Annual Symposium, Cedar Rapids, Iowa, March 27, 1987, 19f.

4. Arnold Mitchell, *The Nine American Lifestyles*, 9–10.

5. Joseph T. Howell, *Hard Living on Clay Street*, 263f.

6. Mitchell, *Nine American Lifestyles*, 6.

7. Ibid., 7–8.

8. Ibid., 5.

9. Ibid., 279.

10. Support for this can be found in studies such as Howell, *Hard Living on Clay Street*; Richard Sennett and Jonathan Cobb, *The Hidden Inquiries of Class* (New York: Vintage Books, 1973); Elliot Liebow, *Tally's Corner*; Gerald D. Suttles, *The Social Order of the Slum*; Kathleen McCourt, *Working Class Women and Grass Roots Politics*; and Lillian B. Rubin, *Worlds of Pain*.

11. Jerry Falwell, *Listen America* (Garden City, N.Y.: Doubleday & Co., 1980). See also John H. Simpson, "Moral Issues and Status Politics," in Robert C. Liebman and Robert Wuthnow, eds., *The New Christian Right*, 188–207.

12. Kenneth A. Briggs, "Evangelicals in America," *Religion in America* (Princeton, N.J.: Gallup Report no. 259, 1987), 4.

13. Robert Booth Fowler, *A New Engagement: Evangelical Political Thought, 1966–1976* (Grand Rapids: Wm. B. Eerdmans Publishing Co., 1982).

14. James Davidson Hunter, "The New Class and The Young Evangelicals," *Review of Religious Research* 22(2):155–169 (Dec. 1980).

15. Nancy T. Ammerman, *Bible Believers*, 8.

16. Wade Clark Roof, "The New Fundamentalism: Rebirth of Political Religion in America," *Prophetic Religions and Politics*, ed. J. K. Hadden and Anson Shupe (New York: Random House, 1986), 20.

17. Samuel S. Hill, "Fundamentalism and the South," *Perspectives in Religious Studies* (Liberty, Mo.: William Jewell College, 1987).

18. Richard Hamilton, *Class and Politics in the United States* (New York: John Wiley & Son, 1972).

19. Beth E. Vanfossen, *The Structure of Social Inequality*, 323.

20. T. W. Adorno et al., *The Authoritarian Personality* (New York: Harper & Row, 1950).

21. Seymour M. Lipset, *Political Man* (Garden City, N.Y.: Double-day & Co., 1960), and "Class Authoritarianism," *American Sociological Review* 24:489.

22. Vanfossen, *Social Inequality*, 342.

23. Lillian B. Rubin, quoted in *Behavior Today*, Dec. 2, 1974, 316; quoted in Vanfossen, *Social Inequality*, 342.

24. Hamilton, *Class and Politics*, 408; quoted in Vanfossen, *Social Inequality*, 343.

25. A. Campbell, *White Attitudes Toward Black People* (Ann Arbor, Mich.: Institute for Social Research, 1971), 49–53; quoted in Vanfossen, *Social Inequality*, 343.

26. Vanfossen, *Social Inequality*, 343.

27. H. E. Ransford, "Blue Collar Anger: Reactions to Student and Black Protest," *American Sociological Review* 37, ch. 8; P. C. Secton and B. Secton, *Blue Collars and Hard Hats* (New York: Random House, 1971), ch. 3. Both are quoted in Vanfossen, *Social Inequality*, 343–344.

28. J. DeFronzo, "Embourgeoisement in Indianapolis?" *Social Problems*, 21:269–283 (1973). Quoted in Vanfossen, *Social Inequality*, 343. See also Wm. P. O'Hare, "Poverty in America: Trends and New Patterns," *Population Bulletin* (June 1985). O'Hare's more recent work demonstrates conclusively that government assistance goes far more to those in the upper strata than those who are poor.

29. Mitchell, *Nine American Lifestyles*, 280.

30. Rebecca Klatch, "Coalition and Conflict Among Women of the New Right," *Signs* 13(4):675 (1988).

31. Ibid., 676.

Chapter 6
Doing Ministry on the Cultural Right

1. Harry C. Boyte, *The Backyard Revolution* (Philadelphia: Temple University Press, 1980), 98.

2. See his *The Idea of Disarmament!* (Elgin, Ill.: Brethren Press, 1982) for a treatment of nuclear weaponry that takes love of country seriously without excluding other nations and peoples.

3. Walter Wink, *Naming the Powers* (Philadelphia: Fortress Press, 1984), 129.

4. John Schaar, quoted in Paul Levy, *Queen Village: The Eclipse of Community* (Philadelphia: Institute for the Study of Civic Values, 1978), 76; quoted in Boyte, *Backyard Revolution*, 23.

5. Richard Flacks, "Making History vs. Making Life—Dilemma of

an American Left," *Working Papers for a New Society* (summer 1974), 60; quoted in Boyte, *Backyard Revolution*, 180.

6. Jerome L. Himmelstein, "The Social Basis of Antifeminism: Religious Networks and Culture," *Journal for the Scientific Study of Religion* 25(1):9 (1986).

7. Ibid., 10.

8. Ibid., 12.

Chapter 7
Popular Religion and Folk Theology

1. Robert Schreiter, *Constructing Local Theologies*, 87–91.

2. Ibid., chapter 6.

3. Ibid., 124.

4. Ibid., 126.

5. Ibid., 127–131.

6. See Clyde Wilcox, "Evangelicals and Fundamentalists in the New Christian Right: Religious Differences in the Ohio Moral Majority," *Journal for the Scientific Study of Religion* 25(2):355–363 (Sept. 1986). Anson Shupe and William A. Stacy, "Public and Clergy Sentiments Toward the Moral Majority: Evidence from the Dallas–Ft. Worth Complex," in D. G. Bromley and Anson Shupe, eds., *New Christian Politics* (Macon, Ga.: Mercer University Press, 1984), 91–100. Stephen D. Johnson and Joseph B. Tamney, "The Christian Right and the 1984 Presidential Election," *Review of Religious Research* 27(2):124–133 (Dec. 1985).

7. Karl Marx and Frederick Engels, *On Religion* (Moscow: Foreign Languages Publishing House, 1957).

8. Schreiter, *Constructing Local Theologies*, 141.

9. Eugene D. Genovese, *Roll, Jordan, Roll* (New York: Vintage Books, 1976).

10. Schreiter, *Constructing Local Theologies*, 80–85.

11. R. Lawrence Moore, *Religious Outsiders and the Making of Americans* (New York: Oxford University Press, 1986).

12. Yoshio Fukuyama, "The Major Dimensions of Church Membership," *Review of Religious Research* 2(4):154ff. (Spring 1961).

13. In this connection see James Ault's study of an independent fundamentalist Baptist church in New England to understand further the dynamics of belief and their role in family relationships: "Family and Fundamentalism: The Shawmut Valley Baptist Church," in Ralph Samuels et al., eds., *Disciplines of Faith* (London: Routledge & Kegan Paul, 1987), 13–36.

Chapter 8
The Cultural Middle and the Commitment to Career

1. Lillian B. Rubin, *Women of a Certain Age* (New York: Harper & Row, 1979), 108.

2. Cited in Beth E. Vanfossen, *The Structure of Social Inequality*, 306f.

3. L. I. Pearlin and M. L. Kohn, "Social Class, Occupation, and Parental Values: A Cross-National Study," *American Sociological Review*, 31:466–479 (1974). Quoted in Vanfossen, *Social Inequality*, 308.

4. Arnold Mitchell, "Nine American Lifestyles," *The Futurist*, August 1984, 5.

5. Arnold Mitchell, *The Nine American Lifestyles*, 178.

6. Ibid., 279.

7. Ibid., 11.

8. Ibid., 279.

9. Ibid., 12.

10. Ibid.

11. Vanfossen, *Social Inequality*, 320f.

12. Ibid., 309.

13. Ibid.

14. W. H. Whyte, Jr., "The Wives of Management," *Fortune* 44:86–87 (1951). Cited in Vanfossen, *Social Inequality*, 310–311.

15. R. M. Kantner, *Men and Women of the Corporation* (New York: Basic Books, 1977), 113–119. Cited in Vanfossen, *Social Inequality*, 308–309.

16. Vanfossen, *Social Inequality*, 311.

17. Ibid., 311–312.

18. Mitchell, *Nine American Lifestyles*, 280.

19. Ibid., 14.

20. S. A. Stouffer, *Communism, Conformity, and Civil Liberties* (Garden City: N.Y.: Doubleday & Co., 1955). Cited in Vanfossen, *Social Inequality*, 304.

21. Vanfossen, *Social Inequality*, 305.

22. Herbert J. Gans, *The Levittowners* (New York: Random House, 1967), 31.

23. Mitchell, *Nine American Lifestyles*, 280.

24. Alexis de Tocqueville, *Democracy in America*, vol. 2, tr. Henry Reeve, rev. Francis Bowen and Phillips Bradley (New York: Vintage Books, 1960), 104–106. For a more recent treatment of some of these issues see Bellah et al., *Habits of the Heart*, 142–163.

Chapter 9
The Cultural Middle and Mainline Churches

1. Max Weber, "The Sociology of Religion," in *From Max Weber: Essays in Sociology*, tr. and ed. by Hans H. Gerth and C. Wright Mills (New York: Oxford University Press, 1958), 271.

2. H. Richard Niebuhr, *The Social Sources of Denominationalism*, 80–81.

3. Ibid., 81–82.

4. Ibid., 83–84.

5. Ibid., 86.

6. Ibid., 86f.

7. Ibid., 87f.

8. Ibid., 88–89.

9. David A. Roozen, William McKinney, and Jackson W. Carroll, *Varieties of Religious Presence*, 100–144.

10. Ibid., 251.

11. Ibid., 252.

12. John Murray Cuddihy, *No Offense: Civil Religion and Protestant Taste*, 27. Quoted in Roozen et al., *Varieties*, 252.

13. Roozen et al., *Varieties*, 253.

14. See, e.g., Charles A. Valentine, *Culture and Poverty* (Chicago: University of Chicago Press, 1968). For a more recent review of the data, see Wm. P. O'Hare, "Poverty in America: Trends and New Patterns," *Population Bulletin* (June 1985), 1–4 and 10–13.

15. George Gallup, Jr., "Commentary," *Religion in America* (Princeton: Gallup Report no. 222, 1984), 5.

16. Roozen et al., *Varieties*, 253.

17. Robert J. Schreiter, *Constructing Local Theologies*, 138.

18. J. Clifford Tharp, Jr., "The Values and Life-Styles of Southern Baptists," *Quarterly Review*, Jan., Feb., March 1988, 58f.

19. "Valscene," Research Service Department of the Southern Baptist Church, Feb. 6, 1987, 2.

20. Warren J. Hartman and Robert L. Wilson, *The Large Membership Church* (Nashville: Abingdon Press, 1989), 16f.

21. J. Clifford Tharp, Jr., "The VALS Lifestyles—Who's Reaching Them?" *Research Information Report*, series 3, no. 1, Research Services Department of the Southern Baptist Church (Feb. 1988), 2.

22. Tharp, "Values and Life-Styles of Southern Baptists," 58.

23. Ibid.

Chapter 10
Cultural-Middle Pain and Explanatory Theology

1. David A. Roozen, William McKinney, and Jackson W. Carroll, *Varieties of Religious Presence*, 248.

2. Ibid., 248–251.

3. See, for example, Rosalind Forbes, *Corporate Stress* (Garden City, N.Y.: Doubleday & Co., 1979), and Michael T. Matteson and John M. Ivancevich, *Managing Job Stress and Health* (New York: Free Press, 1982), and listen to a physician, who, after addressing the issue of stress and unemployment, offers two possible answers but concludes as one might expect in a society where too much injustice is laid finally at the door of the individual.

"Despite my seeming pessimism [about stress caused by unemployment], there *are* ways of assisting both individuals and groups to cope with threatened and actual unemployment with job loss and lay-off.... In some instances, appropriate career counseling and preparation for jobs which *are* in demand can solve the problem. At the other extreme the solution will require legislation to ensure full employment with major sacrifices on the part of some for the betterment of all. *The simple recognition* that we will *continue to live in a climate of underemployment* which will *affect all workers at all levels—and the acceptance of that fact—becomes important to all.*" Alan A. McLean, *Work Stress* (Reading, Mass.: Addison-Wesley Publishing Co., 1979), 56.

4. Paul Tillich, *Systematic Theology*, vol. 3 (Chicago: University of Chicago Press, 1963), 394–433.

5. Robert J. Schreiter, *Constructing Local Theologies*, 87.

6. Tillich, *Systematic Theology*, vol. 1, 8–11.

7. Schreiter, *Constructing Local Theologies*, 88–89.

8. Clifford Geertz, *The Interpretation of Cultures* (New York: Basic Books, 1973), 3–30.

9. Roozen et al., *Varieties*, 248.

10. Jürgen Moltmann, *The Crucified God* (New York: Harper & Row, 1974), 333, 334, 335.

Chapter 11
The Church and Diverse Lifestyles

1. My colleague Eugene L. Lowry has been especially helpful in addressing narrative preaching. His work bodes well indeed for an approach that can reach persons across diverse lifestyles. See his *The Homiletical Plot* (Atlanta: John Knox Press, 1980) and *Doing Time in the Pulpit* (Nashville: Abingdon Press, 1985).

2. Lyle Schaller, *Assimilating New Members* (Nashville: Abingdon Press, 1978), 95.

3. Lyle Schaller, *Growing Plans* (Nashville: Abingdon Press, 1983), 115–116.

4. Ibid., 98–102.

5. Charles H. Bayer, *A Guide to Liberation Theology for Middle Class Congregations* (St. Louis: CBP Press, 1986), 67.

6. Ibid., 136f.

7. Ibid., 130–151.

8. Ibid., 63.

Chapter 12
The Christ in Culture Transforming Culture

1. H. Richard Niebuhr, *Christ and Culture* (New York: Harper & Row, 1951), 11.

2. Ibid., 40–44.

3. Among the important treatments of John's Gospel, see C. K. Barrett, *The Gospel According to John* (London: SPCK, 1967); R. Brown, *The Gospel According to John*, 2 vols. (Garden City, N.Y.: Doubleday & Co., 1966–70); Elisabeth Schüssler Fiorenza, *In Memory of Her* (New York: Crossroad Publishing Co., 1983), 323–342; E. Hoskyns, *The Fourth Gospel* (London: Faber & Faber, 1947); and Rudolf Bultmann, *The Gospel of John: A Commentary*, Eng. tr. G. R. Beasley Murray et al. (Philadelphia: Westminster Press, 1971).

Selected
Bibliography

Ammerman, Nancy T. *Bible Believers*. New Brunswick, N.J.: Rutgers University Press, 1987.

Bayer, Charles H. *A Guide to Liberation Theology for Middle Class Congregations*. St. Louis: CBP Press, 1986.

Bellah, Robert, et al. *Habits of the Heart: Individualism and Commitment in American Life*. Berkeley, Calif.: University of California Press, 1985.

Cuddihy, John Murray. *No Offense: Civil Religion and Protestant Taste*. New York: Seabury Press, 1978.

Hoge, Dean R., and David A. Roozen, eds. *Understanding Church Growth and Decline 1950–1978*. New York: Pilgrim Press, 1979.

Howell, Joseph T. *Hard Living on Clay Street*. Garden City, N.Y.: Doubleday & Co., Anchor Books, 1973.

Liebman, Robert C., and Robert Wuthnow, eds. *The New Christian Right*. New York: Aldine Publishing Co., 1983.

Liebow, Elliot. *Tally's Corner*. Boston: Little, Brown & Co., 1967.

McCourt, Kathleen. *Working Class Women and Grass Roots Politics*. Bloomington, Ind.: Indiana University Press, 1977.

Mills, C. Wright. *White Collar: The American Middle Classes*. New York: Oxford University Press, 1951.

Mitchell, Arnold. *The Nine American Lifestyles*. New York: Warner Books, 1983.

Niebuhr, H. Richard. *The Social Sources of Denominationalism*. New York: Meridian Books, 1957.

Riesman, David, et al. *The Lonely Crowd*. New Haven, Conn.: Yale University Press, 1950.

Roof, Wade Clark, and William McKinney. *American Mainline Religion*. New Brunswick, N.J.: Rutgers University Press, 1987.

Roozen, David A., William McKinney, and Jackson W. Carroll. *Varieties of Religious Presence*. New York: Pilgrim Press, 1984.

Rubin, Lillian B. *Worlds of Pain*. New York: Basic Books, 1976.

Sample, Tex. *Blue Collar Ministry*. Valley Forge, Pa.: Judson Press, 1984.

Schreiter, Robert J. *Constructing Local Theologies*. Maryknoll, N.Y.: Orbis Books, 1985.

Suttles, Gerald D. *The Social Order of the Slum*. Chicago: University of Chicago Press, 1968.

Vanfossen, Beth E. *The Structure of Social Inequality.* Boston: Little, Brown & Co., 1979.

Yankelovich, Daniel. *New Rules: Searching for Self-Fulfillment in a World Turned Upside Down.* New York: Random House, 1981.

Index

Adorno, T. W., 64
affluence, psychology of, 16, 20
Alban Institute, 37
Alcoholics Anonymous, 93
Ammerman, Nancy T., 63

baby boomers: income, 19, 50, 102;
    relation to institutional life, 49, 50,
    122, 143; religious expression, 18;
    values, 19; yuppies 50, 102
Bayer, Charles H., 146

career: and culture, 149–151; and
    lifestyles, 71, 101, 110, 128–129
Carrigan, Robert, 110
Carroll, Jackson W., 117, 118, 125–126,
    133
Christ: and culture 149, 151; in
    differing lifestyles, 42–43
Christ-in-culture, 151–154
church administration, in differing
    lifestyles, 142–145, 147
church participation: and baby
    boomers, 32, 122; and cultural right,
    62, 64, 91; and self-denial ethic, 17;
    and self-fulfillment ethic, 17
churches: conservative, 18; Greek
    Orthodox, 122; mainline, 131, 141,
    145; middle-class, 116, 118, 120,
    146–147; occupations represented,
    121–122; Reorganized Church of
    Latter Day Saints, 140; Roman
    Catholic, 122, 131; Southern Baptist
    Convention, 121, 122; United
    Methodist, 121
civil rights movement: and baby
    boomers, 48, 50; and cultural
    middle, 108; and cultural right, 65
Cuddihy, John Murray, 118

cultural left: characteristics of, 25–28,
    31; church programming with, 33–
    36, 143; commitment and
    relationships, 51; education, 28;
    Experientials, 27; fellowship groups
    and, 34, 40; I-Am-Mes, 26; income,
    28, 39; mission of, 34; outreach to,
    36–42; pastoral leadership and, 37;
    size of U.S. population, 25;
    Societally Conscious, 28, 34;
    worship and, 34
cultural middle: activism of, 123, 125–
    126; baby boomers, 102, 111; career
    and, 101, 110, 128–129, 131;
    characteristics of, 101–112; church
    programming with, 144–145;
    Conflicted, 104–105, 107, 109, 141;
    education, 101, 105, 107, 132;
    family, 105–107, 110, 118, 128–129;
    income, 103, 104, 105, 107, 110;
    mission of, 116, 117, 124–125;
    pastoral care needs, 126; political
    views, 108–109; race and, 103, 104;
    religious expression of, 113–117,
    120, 141; size of U.S. population,
    103; social change strategies with,
    117, 119, 125–126, 129, 146–147;
    stress, 127–128, 133; Strivers, 104,
    107, 109, 122, 129; Successfuls, 103,
    107, 121, 129, 141; women, 105–106;
    works righteousness, 127–128, 133
cultural right: career and, 58; church
    administration style with, 91;
    church participation, 62; church
    programming, 143–144; class status,
    59, 60; Desperate Poor, 61, 62, 64;
    education and, 58, 70, 83–84; ethnic
    groups, 61, 66; family and, 67, 71,
    72, 91; Hard Living types, 60, 64;

169